FROM THE EDITOR

Digital LSAT™

In North America the LSAT is now delivered in a digital format, on tablets instead of in test books. The Digital LSAT differs from the paper-and-pencil LSAT test book in delivery method only—the content is the same, as is the structure of the test sections. To learn more about the LSAT, visit our website, LSAC.org.

LSAT Writing™

The LSAT includes an unscored writing section. While the writing section was historically administered on the same day as the multiple choice sections, it is now administered on a secure, proctored online platform at a time and place of the candidate's choosing. LSAT Writing differs from the paper-and-pencil Writing Sample in delivery method only. To learn more about LSAT Writing, visit our website, LSAC.org.

The Law School Admission Council is a not-for-profit organization committed to promoting quality, access, and equity in law and education worldwide by supporting individuals' enrollment journeys and providing preeminent assessment, data, and technology services. Currently, 221 law schools in the United States, Canada, and Australia are members of the Council and benefit from LSAC's services.

©2019 Law School Admission Council, Inc.

LSAT, Law School Admission Test, *The Official LSAT PrepTest, The Official LSAT SuperPrep,* and LSAC are registered marks of the Law School Admission Council, Inc. Law School Forums, Credential Assembly Service, CAS, LLM Credential Assembly Service, and LLM CAS are service marks of the Law School Admission Council, Inc. Digital LSAT; LSAT Writing; *10 Actual, Official LSAT PrepTests; 10 More Actual, Official LSAT PrepTests; The Next 10 Actual, Official LSAT PrepTests; 10 Actual, Official LSAT PrepTests 42–51; 10 New Actual, Official LSAT PrepTests with Comparative Reading; 10 Actual, Official LSAT PrepTests, Volume V; 10 Actual, Official LSAT PrepTests, Volume VI; The Official LSAT SuperPrep II;* LSAC Official Guide to ABA-Approved Law Schools; LSAC Official Guide to LLM/Graduate Law Programs; *The Official LSAT Handbook*; ACES²; FlexApp; Candidate Referral Service; and Law School Admission Council are trademarks of the Law School Admission Council, Inc.

All rights reserved. No part of this work, including information, data, or other portions of the work published in electronic form, may be reproduced or transmitted in any form or by any means, electronic or mechanical, including photocopying, recording, or by any information storage and retrieval system, without permission of the publisher. For information, write: Assessment Publications, Law School Admission Council, 662 Penn Street, PO Box 40, Newtown, PA 18940-0040.

LSAC fees, policies, and procedures relating to, but not limited to, test registration, test administration, test score reporting, misconduct and irregularities, Credential Assembly Service (CAS), and other matters may change without notice at any time. Up-to-date LSAC policies and procedures are available at LSAC.org.

ISBN-13: 978-0-9996580-8-6

Print number

10 9 8 7 6 5 4 3 2 1

TABLE OF CONTENTS

- Introduction to the LSAT 1
  - Scoring 1
    - Test Score Accuracy—Reliability and Standard Error of Measurement 1
    - Adjustments for Variation in Test Difficulty 1
    - Research on the LSAT 1
  - How This PrepTest Differs From an Actual LSAT 2
  - The Three LSAT Multiple-Choice Question Types 2
    - Analytical Reasoning Questions 2
    - Logical Reasoning Questions 3
    - Reading Comprehension Questions 4
  - Taking the PrepTest Under Simulated LSAT Conditions 5
- Answer Sheet 7
- The PrepTest 9
- Computing Your Score 43
- Answer Key 44

INTRODUCTION TO THE LSAT

The Law School Admission Test is an integral part of law school admission in the United States, Canada, and a growing number of other countries. The LSAT is the only test accepted for admission purposes by all ABA-accredited law schools and Canadian common-law law schools. It consists of five 35-minute sections of multiple-choice questions. Four of the five sections contribute to the test taker's score. These sections include one Reading Comprehension section, one Analytical Reasoning section, and two Logical Reasoning sections. The unscored section, commonly referred to as the variable section, typically is used to pretest new test questions or to preequate new test forms. The placement of this section in the LSAT will vary. The score scale for the LSAT is 120 to 180.

The LSAT is designed to measure skills considered essential for success in law school: the reading and comprehension of complex texts with accuracy and insight; the organization and management of information and the ability to draw reasonable inferences from it; the ability to think critically; and the analysis and evaluation of the reasoning and arguments of others.

The LSAT provides a standard measure of acquired reading and verbal reasoning skills that law schools can use as one of several factors in assessing applicants.

For up-to-date information about LSAC's services, go to our website, LSAC.org.

SCORING

Your LSAT score is based on the number of questions you answer correctly (the raw score). There is no deduction for incorrect answers, and all questions count equally. In other words, there is no penalty for guessing.

Test Score Accuracy—Reliability and Standard Error of Measurement

Candidates perform at different levels on different occasions for reasons quite unrelated to the characteristics of a test itself. The accuracy of test scores is best described by the use of two related statistical terms: reliability and standard error of measurement.

Reliability is a measure of how consistently a test measures the skills being assessed. The higher the reliability coefficient for a test, the more certain we can be that test takers would get very similar scores if they took the test again.

LSAC reports an internal consistency measure of reliability for every test form. Reliability can vary from 0.00 to 1.00, and a test with no measurement error would have a reliability coefficient of 1.00 (never attained in practice). Reliability coefficients for past LSAT forms have ranged from .90 to .95, indicating a high degree of consistency for these tests. LSAC expects the reliability of the LSAT to continue to fall within the same range.

LSAC also reports the amount of measurement error associated with each test form, a concept known as the standard error of measurement (SEM). The SEM, which is usually about 2.6 points, indicates how close a test taker's observed score is likely to be to their true score. True scores are theoretical scores that would be obtained from perfectly reliable tests with no measurement error—scores never known in practice.

Score bands, or ranges of scores that contain a test taker's true score a certain percentage of the time, can be derived using the SEM. LSAT score bands are constructed by adding and subtracting the (rounded) SEM to and from an actual LSAT score (e.g., the LSAT score, plus or minus 3 points). Scores near 120 or 180 have asymmetrical bands. Score bands constructed in this manner will contain an individual's true score approximately 68 percent of the time.

Measurement error also must be taken into account when comparing LSAT scores of two test takers. It is likely that small differences in scores are due to measurement error rather than to meaningful differences in ability. The standard error of score differences provides some guidance as to the importance of differences between two scores. The standard error of score differences is approximately 1.4 times larger than the standard error of measurement for the individual scores.

Thus, a test score should be regarded as a useful but approximate measure of a test taker's abilities as measured by the test, not as an exact determination of those abilities. LSAC encourages law schools to examine the range of scores within the interval that probably contains the test taker's true score (e.g., the test taker's score band) rather than solely interpret the reported score alone.

Adjustments for Variation in Test Difficulty

All test forms of the LSAT reported on the same score scale are designed to measure the same abilities, but one test form may be slightly easier or more difficult than another. The scores from different test forms are made comparable through a statistical procedure known as equating. As a result of equating, a given scaled score earned on different test forms reflects the same level of ability.

Research on the LSAT

Summaries of LSAT validity studies and other LSAT research can be found in member law school libraries and at LSAC.org.

HOW THIS PREPTEST DIFFERS FROM AN ACTUAL LSAT

This PrepTest is made up of the scored sections from the actual disclosed LSAT administered in November 2019. However, it does not contain the extra, variable section that is used to pretest new test items of one of the three multiple-choice question types. The three multiple-choice question types may be in a different order in an actual LSAT than in this PrepTest. This is because the order of these question types is intentionally varied for each administration of the test.

THE THREE LSAT MULTIPLE-CHOICE QUESTION TYPES

The multiple-choice questions on the LSAT reflect a broad range of academic disciplines and are intended to give no advantage to candidates from a particular academic background.

The five sections of the test contain three different question types. The following material presents a general discussion of the nature of each question type and some strategies that can be used in answering them.

Analytical Reasoning Questions

Analytical Reasoning questions are designed to assess the ability to consider a group of facts and rules, and, given those facts and rules, determine what could or must be true. The specific scenarios associated with these questions are usually unrelated to law, since they are intended to be accessible to a wide range of test takers. However, the skills tested parallel those involved in determining what could or must be the case given a set of regulations, the terms of a contract, or the facts of a legal case in relation to the law. In Analytical Reasoning questions, you are asked to reason deductively from a set of statements and rules or principles that describe relationships among persons, things, or events.

Analytical Reasoning questions appear in sets, with each set based on a single passage. The passage used for each set of questions describes common ordering relationships or grouping relationships, or a combination of both types of relationships. Examples include scheduling employees for work shifts, assigning instructors to class sections, ordering tasks according to priority, and distributing grants for projects.

Analytical Reasoning questions test a range of deductive reasoning skills. These include:

- Comprehending the basic structure of a set of relationships by determining a complete solution to the problem posed (for example, an acceptable seating arrangement of all six diplomats around a table)

- Reasoning with conditional ("if-then") statements and recognizing logically equivalent formulations of such statements

- Inferring what could be true or must be true from given facts and rules

- Inferring what could be true or must be true from given facts and rules together with new information in the form of an additional or substitute fact or rule

- Recognizing when two statements are logically equivalent in context by identifying a condition or rule that could replace one of the original conditions while still resulting in the same possible outcomes

Analytical Reasoning questions reflect the kinds of detailed analyses of relationships and sets of constraints that a law student must perform in legal problem solving. For example, an Analytical Reasoning passage might describe six diplomats being seated around a table, following certain rules of protocol as to who can sit where. You, the test taker, must answer questions about the logical implications of given and new information. For example, you may be asked who can sit between diplomats X and Y, or who cannot sit next to X if W sits next to Y. Similarly, if you were a student in law school, you might be asked to analyze a scenario involving a set of particular circumstances and a set of governing rules in the form of constitutional provisions, statutes, administrative codes, or prior rulings that have been upheld. You might then be asked to determine the legal options in the scenario: what is required given the scenario, what is permissible given the scenario, and what is prohibited given the scenario. Or you might be asked to develop a "theory" for the case: when faced with an incomplete set of facts about the case, you must fill in the picture based on what is implied by the facts that are known. The problem could be elaborated by the addition of new information or hypotheticals.

No formal training in logic is required to answer these questions correctly. Analytical Reasoning questions are intended to be answered using knowledge, skills, and reasoning ability generally expected of college students and graduates.

Suggested Approach

Some people may prefer to answer first those questions about a passage that seem less difficult and then those that seem more difficult. In general, it is best to finish one passage before starting on another, because much time can be lost in returning to a passage and reestablishing familiarity with its relationships. However, if you are having great difficulty on one particular set of questions and are spending too much time on them, it may be to your advantage to skip that set of questions and go on to the next passage, returning to the problematic set of questions after you have finished the other questions in the section.

Do not assume that because the conditions for a set of questions look long or complicated, the questions based on those conditions will be especially difficult.

Read the passage carefully. Careful reading and analysis are necessary to determine the exact nature of the relationships involved in an Analytical Reasoning passage. Some relationships are fixed (for example, P and R must always work on the same project). Other relationships are variable (for example, Q must be assigned to either team 1 or team 3). Some relationships that are not stated explicitly in the conditions are implied by and can be deduced from those that are stated (for example, if one condition about paintings in a display specifies that Painting K must be to the left of Painting Y, and another specifies that Painting W must be to the left of Painting K, then it can be deduced that Painting W must be to the left of Painting Y).

In reading the conditions, do not introduce unwarranted assumptions. For instance, in a set of questions establishing relationships of height and weight among the members of a team, do not assume that a person who is taller than another person must weigh more than that person. As another example, suppose a set involves ordering and a question in the set asks what must be true if both X and Y must be earlier than Z; in this case, do not assume that X must be earlier than Y merely because X is mentioned before Y. All the information needed to answer each question is provided in the passage and the question itself.

The conditions are designed to be as clear as possible. Do not interpret the conditions as if they were intended to trick you. For example, if a question asks how many people could be eligible to serve on a committee, consider only those people named in the passage unless directed otherwise. When in doubt, read the conditions in their most obvious sense. Remember, however, that the language in the conditions is intended to be read for precise meaning. It is essential to pay particular attention to words that describe or limit relationships, such as "only," "exactly," "never," "always," "must be," "cannot be," and the like.

The result of this careful reading will be a clear picture of the structure of the relationships involved, including the kinds of relationships permitted, the participants in the relationships, and the range of possible actions or attributes for these participants.

Keep in mind question independence. Each question should be considered separately from the other questions in its set. No information, except what is given in the original conditions, should be carried over from one question to another.

In some cases a question will simply ask for conclusions to be drawn from the conditions as originally given. Some questions may, however, add information to the original conditions or temporarily suspend or replace one of the original conditions for the purpose of that question only. For example, if Question 1 adds the supposition "if P is sitting at table 2 ...," this supposition should NOT be carried over to any other question in the set.

Logical Reasoning Questions

Arguments are a fundamental part of the law, and analyzing arguments is a key element of legal analysis. Training in the law builds on a foundation of basic reasoning skills. Law students must draw on the skills of analyzing, evaluating, constructing, and refuting arguments. They need to be able to identify what information is relevant to an issue or argument and what impact further evidence might have. They need to be able to reconcile opposing positions and use arguments to persuade others.

Logical Reasoning questions evaluate the ability to analyze, critically evaluate, and complete arguments as they occur in ordinary language. The questions are based on short arguments drawn from a wide variety of sources, including newspapers, general interest magazines, scholarly publications, advertisements, and informal discourse. These arguments mirror legal reasoning in the types of arguments presented and in their complexity, though few of the arguments actually have law as a subject matter.

Each Logical Reasoning question requires you to read and comprehend a short passage, then answer one question (or, rarely, two questions) about it. The questions are designed to assess a wide range of skills involved in thinking critically, with an emphasis on skills that are central to legal reasoning.

These skills include:

- Recognizing the parts of an argument and their relationships

- Recognizing similarities and differences between patterns of reasoning

- Drawing well-supported conclusions

- Reasoning by analogy

- Recognizing misunderstandings or points of disagreement

- Determining how additional evidence affects an argument

- Detecting assumptions made by particular arguments

- Identifying and applying principles or rules

- Identifying flaws in arguments

- Identifying explanations

The questions do not presuppose specialized knowledge of logical terminology. For example, you will not be expected to know the meaning of specialized terms such as "ad hominem" or "syllogism." On the other hand, you will be expected to understand and critique the reasoning contained in arguments. This requires that you possess a university-level understanding of widely used concepts such as argument, premise, assumption, and conclusion.

Suggested Approach
Read each question carefully. Make sure that you understand the meaning of each part of the question. Make sure that you understand the meaning of each answer choice and the ways in which it may or may not relate to the question posed.

Do not pick a response simply because it is a true statement. Although true, it may not answer the question posed.

Answer each question on the basis of the information that is given, even if you do not agree with it. Work within the context provided by the passage. LSAT questions do not involve any tricks or hidden meanings.

Reading Comprehension Questions

Both law school and the practice of law revolve around extensive reading of highly varied, dense, argumentative, and expository texts (for example, cases, codes, contracts, briefs, decisions, evidence). This reading must be exacting, distinguishing precisely what is said from what is not said. It involves comparison, analysis, synthesis, and application (for example, of principles and rules). It involves drawing appropriate inferences and applying ideas and arguments to new contexts. Law school reading also requires the ability to grasp unfamiliar subject matter and the ability to penetrate difficult and challenging material.

The purpose of LSAT Reading Comprehension questions is to measure the ability to read, with understanding and insight, examples of lengthy and complex materials similar to those commonly encountered in law school. The Reading Comprehension section of the LSAT contains four sets of reading questions, each set consisting of a selection of reading material followed by five to eight questions. The reading selection in three of the four sets consists of a single reading passage; the other set contains two related shorter passages. Sets with two passages are a variant of Reading Comprehension called Comparative Reading, which was introduced in June 2007.

Comparative Reading questions concern the relationships between the two passages, such as those of generalization/instance, principle/application, or point/counterpoint. Law school work often requires reading two or more texts in conjunction with each other and understanding their relationships. For example, a law student may read a trial court decision together with an appellate court decision that overturns it, or identify the fact pattern from a hypothetical suit together with the potentially controlling case law.

Reading selections for LSAT Reading Comprehension questions are drawn from a wide range of subjects in the humanities, the social sciences, the biological and physical sciences, and areas related to the law. Generally, the selections are densely written, use high-level vocabulary, and contain sophisticated argument or complex rhetorical structure (for example, multiple points of view). Reading Comprehension questions require you to read carefully and accurately, to determine the relationships among the various parts of the reading selection, and to draw reasonable inferences from the material in the selection. The questions may ask about the following characteristics of a passage or pair of passages:

- The main idea or primary purpose

- Information that is explicitly stated

- Information or ideas that can be inferred

- The meaning or purpose of words or phrases as used in context

- The organization or structure

- The application of information in the selection to a new context

- Principles that function in the selection

- Analogies to claims or arguments in the selection

- An author's attitude as revealed in the tone of a passage or the language used

- The impact of new information on claims or arguments in the selection

Suggested Approach
Since reading selections are drawn from many different disciplines and sources, you should not be discouraged if you encounter material with which you are not familiar. It is important to remember that questions are to be answered exclusively on the basis of the information provided in the selection. There is no particular knowledge that you are expected to bring to the test, and you should not make inferences based on any prior knowledge of a subject that you may have. You may, however, wish to defer working on a set of questions that seems particularly difficult or unfamiliar until after you have dealt with sets you find easier.

Strategies. One question that often arises in connection with Reading Comprehension has to do with the most effective and efficient order in which to read the selections and questions. Possible approaches include:

- reading the selection very closely and then answering the questions;

- reading the questions first, reading the selection closely, and then returning to the questions; or

- skimming the selection and questions very quickly, then rereading the selection closely and answering the questions.

Test takers are different, and the best strategy for one might not be the best strategy for another. In preparing for the test, therefore, you might want to experiment with the different strategies and decide what works most effectively for you.

Remember that your strategy must be effective under timed conditions. For this reason, the first strategy—reading the selection very closely and then answering the questions—may be the most effective for you. Nonetheless, if you believe that one of the other strategies might be more effective for you, you should try it out and assess your performance using it.

Reading the selection. Whatever strategy you choose, you should give the passage or pair of passages at least one careful reading before answering the questions. Try to distinguish main ideas from supporting ideas, and opinions or attitudes from factual, objective information. Note transitions from one idea to the next and identify the relationships among the different ideas or parts of a passage, or between the two passages in Comparative Reading sets. Consider how and why an author makes points and draws conclusions. Be sensitive to implications of what the passages say.

You may find it helpful to mark key parts of passages. For example, you might underline main ideas or important arguments, and you might note transitional words—"although," "nevertheless," "correspondingly," and the like—that will help you map the structure of a passage. Also, you might note descriptive words that will help you identify an author's attitude toward a particular idea or person.

Answering the Questions

- Always read all the answer choices before selecting the best answer. The best answer choice is the one that most accurately and completely answers the question being posed.

- Respond to the specific question being asked. Do not pick an answer choice simply because it is a true statement. For example, picking a true statement might yield an incorrect answer to a question in which you are asked to identify an author's position on an issue, since you are not being asked to evaluate the truth of the author's position but only to correctly identify what that position is.

- Answer the questions only on the basis of the information provided in the selection. Your own views, interpretations, or opinions, and those you have heard from others, may sometimes conflict with those expressed in a reading selection; however, you are expected to work within the context provided by the reading selection. You should not expect to agree with everything you encounter in Reading Comprehension passages.

TAKING THE PRETEST UNDER SIMULATED LSAT CONDITIONS

One important way to prepare for the LSAT is to simulate the day of the test by taking a practice test under actual time constraints. Taking a practice test under timed conditions helps you to estimate the amount of time you can afford to spend on each question in a section and to determine the question types on which you may need additional practice.

Since the LSAT is a timed test, it is important to use your allotted time wisely. During the test, you may work only on the section designated by the test supervisor. You cannot devote extra time to a difficult section and make up that time on a section you find easier. In pacing yourself, and checking your answers, you should think of each section of the test as a separate minitest.

Be sure that you answer every question on the test. When you do not know the correct answer to a question, first eliminate the responses that you know are incorrect, then make your best guess among the remaining choices. Do not be afraid to guess as there is no penalty for incorrect answers.

When you take a practice test, abide by all the requirements specified in the directions and keep strictly within the specified time limits. Work without a rest period. When you take an actual test, you will have only a short break—usually 10–15 minutes—after Section III.

When taken under conditions as much like actual testing conditions as possible, a practice test provides very useful preparation for taking the LSAT.

Official directions for the four multiple-choice sections are included in this PrepTest so that you can approximate actual testing conditions as you practice.

To take the test:

- Set a timer for 35 minutes. Answer all the questions in Section I of this PrepTest. Stop working on that section when the 35 minutes have elapsed.
- Repeat, allowing yourself 35 minutes each for Sections II, III, and IV.
- Refer to the "Computing Your Score" section at the end of the PrepTest for instruction on evaluating your performance. An answer key is provided for that purpose.

The practice test that follows consists of four sections corresponding to the four scored sections of the November 2019 LSAT.

General Directions for the LSAT Answer Sheet

This portion of the test consists of five multiple-choice sections, each with a time limit of 35 minutes. The supervisor will tell you when to begin and end each section. If you finish a section before time is called, you may check your work on that section **only**; do not turn to any other section of the test book and do not work on any other section either in the test book or on the answer sheet.

There are several different types of questions on the test, and each question type has its own directions. **Be sure you understand the directions for each question type before attempting to answer any questions in that section.**

Not everyone will finish all the questions in the time allowed. Do not hurry, but work steadily and as quickly as you can without sacrificing accuracy. You are advised to use your time effectively. If a question seems too difficult, go on to the next one and return to the difficult question after completing the section. **MARK THE BEST ANSWER YOU CAN FOR EVERY QUESTION. NO DEDUCTIONS WILL BE MADE FOR WRONG ANSWERS. YOUR SCORE WILL BE BASED ONLY ON THE NUMBER OF QUESTIONS YOU ANSWER CORRECTLY.**

ALL YOUR ANSWERS MUST BE MARKED ON THE ANSWER SHEET. Answer spaces for each question are lettered to correspond with the letters of the potential answers to each question in the test book. After you have decided which of the answers is correct, blacken the corresponding space on the answer sheet. **BE SURE THAT EACH MARK IS BLACK AND COMPLETELY FILLS THE ANSWER SPACE.** Give only one answer to each question. If you change an answer, be sure that all previous marks are **erased completely.** Since the answer sheet is machine scored, incomplete erasures may be interpreted as intended answers. **ANSWERS RECORDED IN THE TEST BOOK WILL NOT BE SCORED.**

There may be more question numbers on this answer sheet than there are questions in a section. Do not be concerned, but be certain that the section and number of the question you are answering matches the answer sheet section and question number. Additional answer spaces in any answer sheet section should be left blank. Begin your next section in the number one answer space for that section.

LSAC takes various steps to ensure that answer sheets are returned from test centers in a timely manner for processing. In the unlikely event that an answer sheet is not received, LSAC will permit the examinee either to retest at no additional fee or to receive a refund of his or her LSAT fee. **THESE REMEDIES ARE THE ONLY REMEDIES AVAILABLE IN THE UNLIKELY EVENT THAT AN ANSWER SHEET IS NOT RECEIVED BY LSAC.**

HOW DID YOU PREPARE FOR THE LSAT?
(Select all that apply.)

Responses to this item are voluntary and will be used for statistical research purposes only.

○ By using Khan Academy's official LSAT practice material.
○ By taking the free sample questions and/or free sample LSAT available on LSAC's website.
○ By working through official LSAT *PrepTest* and/or other LSAC test prep products.
○ By using LSAT prep books or software **not** published by LSAC.
○ By attending a commercial test preparation or coaching course.
○ By attending a test preparation or coaching course offered through an undergraduate institution.
○ Self study.
○ Other preparation.
○ No preparation.

CERTIFYING STATEMENT

Please write the following statement. Sign and date.

I certify that I am the examinee whose name appears on this answer sheet and that I am here to take the LSAT for the sole purpose of being considered for admission to law school. I further certify that I will neither assist nor receive assistance from any other candidate, and I agree not to copy, retain, or transmit examination questions in any form or discuss them with any other person.

_____
_____
_____
_____
_____
_____
_____
_____

SIGNATURE: _____   TODAY'S DATE: __/__/__
                                                    MONTH DAY YEAR

DO NOT WRITE IN THIS BOX.

FOR LSAC USE ONLY

THE PREPTEST

- Analytical Reasoning . . . . SECTION I
- Logical Reasoning. . . . . SECTION II
- Reading Comprehension. . . . . SECTION III
- Logical Reasoning. . . . . .SECTION IV

SECTION I
Time—35 minutes
23 Questions

Directions: Each set of questions in this section is based on a scenario with a set of conditions. The questions are to be answered on the basis of what can be logically inferred from the scenario and conditions. For each question, choose the response that most accurately and completely answers the question and mark that response on your answer sheet.

Questions 1–5

A customer service department is scheduling its five agents—Quinn, Rodriguez, Shaw, Tran, and Upton—to attend off-site training sessions being held over a seven-month period, month 1 through month 7. Each agent will be trained in a different month. The training must take place in accordance with the following conditions:
   Month 6 is one of the months in which none of the agents is trained.
   Upton is trained in an earlier month than Rodriguez.
   Quinn is trained in the month immediately before the month in which Tran is trained.
   Shaw is the third agent to be trained.

1. Which one of the following is an acceptable schedule for the training?
    (A) month 1: Quinn
        month 2: Tran
        month 4: Shaw
        month 5: Upton
        month 7: Rodriguez
    (B) month 1: Quinn
        month 2: Tran
        month 5: Shaw
        month 6: Upton
        month 7: Rodriguez
    (C) month 1: Quinn
        month 3: Tran
        month 4: Shaw
        month 5: Upton
        month 7: Rodriguez
    (D) month 1: Upton
        month 3: Shaw
        month 4: Quinn
        month 5: Tran
        month 7: Rodriguez
    (E) month 2: Quinn
        month 3: Tran
        month 4: Shaw
        month 5: Rodriguez
        month 7: Upton

GO ON TO THE NEXT PAGE.

2. If Tran is not trained in month 2, which one of the following could be true?

    (A) Quinn is trained in month 1.
    (B) Rodriguez is trained in month 5.
    (C) Shaw is trained in month 4.
    (D) Upton is trained in month 4.
    (E) None of the agents is trained in month 3.

3. If Shaw is trained in month 4, which one of the following must be true?

    (A) Quinn is trained in month 1.
    (B) Quinn is trained in month 2.
    (C) None of the agents is trained in month 3.
    (D) Upton is trained in month 5.
    (E) None of the agents is trained in month 7.

4. Which one of the following could be the month in which Upton is trained?

    (A) month 2
    (B) month 3
    (C) month 4
    (D) month 6
    (E) month 7

5. Which one of the following is a month in which an agent must be trained?

    (A) month 1
    (B) month 2
    (C) month 3
    (D) month 4
    (E) month 5

GO ON TO THE NEXT PAGE.

Questions 6–12

In creating a soup recipe, a chef is deciding which of seven vegetables—garlic, jalapeño, kale, onion, potato, tomato, and yam—to include among the ingredients. The chef has decided that the vegetables she includes will be added one at a time to a pot of liquid ingredients. Each vegetable will be added only once, subject to the following conditions:

If jalapeño is an ingredient, it must be added either first or last.
If jalapeño is an ingredient, yam must not be an ingredient.
Either potato is an ingredient or yam is an ingredient, but not both.
Garlic, kale, onion, and tomato must be ingredients.
Onion must be added at some time before garlic, and garlic must be added at some time before both kale and tomato.

6. Which one of the following could be the order in which the vegetables are added to the pot, listed from first to last?

(A) onion, garlic, tomato, kale
(B) garlic, onion, kale, tomato, potato
(C) jalapeño, onion, garlic, potato, tomato, kale
(D) onion, garlic, kale, yam, tomato, jalapeño
(E) potato, onion, garlic, kale, jalapeño, tomato

7. Which one of the following could be true?

(A) Garlic is added first.
(B) Garlic is added fifth.
(C) Jalapeño is added fifth.
(D) Potato is added first.
(E) Tomato is added second.

GO ON TO THE NEXT PAGE.

8. If yam is added first, which one of the following must be true?

    (A) Garlic is added second.
    (B) Jalapeño is added fifth.
    (C) Kale is added fourth.
    (D) Onion is added second.
    (E) Tomato is added fifth.

9. Any of the following could be added fourth EXCEPT:

    (A) garlic
    (B) onion
    (C) potato
    (D) tomato
    (E) yam

10. If yam is added fifth, which one of the following could be true?

    (A) Garlic is added third.
    (B) Jalapeño is added first.
    (C) Kale is added third.
    (D) Kale is added sixth.
    (E) Onion is added second.

11. Any of the following could be added sixth EXCEPT:

    (A) jalapeño
    (B) kale
    (C) potato
    (D) tomato
    (E) yam

12. Which one of the following, if substituted for the condition that if jalapeño is an ingredient, yam must not be an ingredient, would have the same effect in determining the addition of vegetables to the pot?

    (A) Potato is an ingredient only if jalapeño is an ingredient.
    (B) Jalapeño is an ingredient only if potato is an ingredient.
    (C) If jalapeño is not an ingredient, then yam must be an ingredient.
    (D) If exactly five vegetables are ingredients, then jalapeño must not be an ingredient.
    (E) If exactly six vegetables are ingredients, then jalapeño must be an ingredient.

GO ON TO THE NEXT PAGE.

Questions 13–17

A computer forensics laboratory is assigning five technicians—Ruiz, Smith, Tapia, Weeks, and Xie—to examine the data on three computers—F, G, and H. Each technician will be assigned to at least one computer, and each computer will be examined by exactly two technicians. The assignment must conform to the following conditions:

    If Smith examines F, Xie examines G.
    If Weeks examines F, Xie examines H.
    No computer is examined by both Smith and Weeks.
    Exactly one computer is examined by both Ruiz and Tapia.

13. Which one of the following is an acceptable assignment of technicians to computers?

(A)   F: Ruiz and Smith
          G: Weeks and Xie
          H: Smith and Tapia

(B)   F: Ruiz and Tapia
          G: Smith and Xie
          H: Smith and Weeks

(C)   F: Ruiz and Tapia
          G: Weeks and Xie
          H: Smith and Xie

(D)   F: Ruiz and Weeks
          G: Smith and Xie
          H: Ruiz and Tapia

(E)   F: Smith and Xie
          G: Ruiz and Tapia
          H: Tapia and Weeks

GO ON TO THE NEXT PAGE.

14. If both Ruiz and Tapia examine G, which one of the following technicians must examine F?

    (A) Ruiz
    (B) Smith
    (C) Tapia
    (D) Weeks
    (E) Xie

15. Any of the following could be true EXCEPT:

    (A) One of the computers is examined by both Ruiz and Xie.
    (B) One of the computers is examined by both Smith and Tapia.
    (C) One of the computers is examined by both Smith and Xie.
    (D) One of the computers is examined by both Tapia and Weeks.
    (E) One of the computers is examined by both Weeks and Xie.

16. If Weeks examines H, then any of the following could be true EXCEPT:

    (A) Ruiz examines H.
    (B) Smith examines F.
    (C) Tapia examines G.
    (D) Tapia examines H.
    (E) Xie examines G.

17. The assignment of technicians to computers is fully determined if which one of the following is true?

    (A) Both Ruiz and Tapia examine G.
    (B) Both Ruiz and Tapia examine H.
    (C) Both Smith and Xie examine G.
    (D) Both Tapia and Weeks examine G.
    (E) Both Weeks and Xie examine H.

GO ON TO THE NEXT PAGE.

Questions 18–23

During the next four months, three factory sites—one in France, one in Ghana, and one in India—will be visited by a company's representatives, exactly one representative for each site in each month. The visits will be made by four representatives—Velez, Watts, Yamamoto, and Zuhur—each of whom will make exactly three visits, no more than one in a month, subject to the following constraints:

Velez must visit Ghana once and India twice, with Ghana visited at some time between the visits to India.
Watts must visit Ghana at least once.
Yamamoto must visit Ghana in a month immediately preceding a month in which Watts visits Ghana.
Yamamoto cannot visit any site in the fourth month.
Any representative who visits France cannot also visit India.

18. Which one of the following could be the representatives who visit France and Ghana, from the first month through the fourth month?

   (A) France: Watts, Yamamoto, Yamamoto, Watts
       Ghana: Yamamoto, Watts, Velez, Zuhur
   (B) France: Watts, Yamamoto, Yamamoto, Watts
       Ghana: Yamamoto, Watts, Zuhur, Velez
   (C) France: Watts, Zuhur, Yamamoto, Watts
       Ghana: Yamamoto, Watts, Velez, Zuhur
   (D) France: Yamamoto, Watts, Watts, Yamamoto
       Ghana: Zuhur, Velez, Yamamoto, Watts
   (E) France: Yamamoto, Watts, Yamamoto, Watts
       Ghana: Watts, Yamamoto, Velez, Zuhur

19. If Velez visits India in the second month, which one of the following must be true?

   (A) Velez visits Ghana in the third month.
   (B) Watts visits France in the second month.
   (C) Watts visits India in the first month.
   (D) Yamamoto visits France in the first month.
   (E) Zuhur visits France in the fourth month.

GO ON TO THE NEXT PAGE.

20. Which one of the following could be true?

    (A) Three of the representatives visit France at least once.
    (B) Three of the representatives visit India at least once.
    (C) One of the representatives visits Ghana two months in a row.
    (D) One of the representatives visits France three months in a row.
    (E) One of the representatives visits India three months in a row.

21. If Zuhur visits France exactly twice, which one of the following must be true?

    (A) Watts visits France exactly twice.
    (B) Watts visits India exactly twice.
    (C) Yamamoto visits India exactly twice.
    (D) Zuhur visits Ghana exactly once.
    (E) Zuhur visits India exactly once.

22. Which one of the following could be true?

    (A) Watts visits Ghana in the first month.
    (B) Yamamoto visits Ghana in the second month.
    (C) Yamamoto visits Ghana in the third month.
    (D) Zuhur visits Ghana in the second month.
    (E) Zuhur visits Ghana in the third month.

23. How many of the representatives are there who could visit a single one of the sites three times?

    (A) zero
    (B) one
    (C) two
    (D) three
    (E) four

S T O P

IF YOU FINISH BEFORE TIME IS CALLED, YOU MAY CHECK YOUR WORK ON THIS SECTION ONLY.
DO NOT WORK ON ANY OTHER SECTION IN THE TEST.

SECTION II
Time—35 minutes
26 Questions

Directions: Each question in this section is based on the reasoning presented in a brief passage. In answering the questions, you should not make assumptions that are by commonsense standards implausible, superfluous, or incompatible with the passage. For some questions, more than one of the choices could conceivably answer the question. However, you are to choose the best answer; that is, choose the response that most accurately and completely answers the question and mark that response on your answer sheet.

1. CEO: While we only have the sales reports for the first 9 months of this year, I feel confident in concluding that this will be a good year for us in terms of sales. In each of the last 5 years, our monthly sales average was less than $30 million. However, our monthly sales average so far for this year is over $35 million.

    Which one of the following, if true, most strengthens the CEO's argument?

    (A) The CEO's company typically has its highest monthly sales of the year during the last 3 months of the year.
    (B) The quality of the products sold by the CEO's company has always been considered to be relatively high.
    (C) The CEO has a strong incentive to highlight any good news regarding the company and to downplay bad news.
    (D) The CEO's company started a new advertising campaign at the beginning of this year that has proved unusually effective so far.
    (E) Several other companies who sell products similar to those sold by the CEO's company have also reported that this year's monthly sales averages so far have been higher than previous years' averages.

2. Javier: Government workers are paid higher hourly wages than comparable private sector employees. So the government could save money by hiring private contractors to perform services now performed by government employees.

    Mykayla: An analysis of government contracts showed that, on average, the government paid substantially more to hire contractors than it would have cost for government employees to perform comparable services.

    Javier and Mykayla disagree with each other over whether

    (A) the government could reduce spending by reducing the number of employees on its payroll
    (B) the government would save money if it hired private contractors to perform services now performed by government employees
    (C) government workers generally are paid higher hourly wages than comparable private sector workers
    (D) every service that is currently performed by government employees could be performed by private contractors
    (E) the total amount of money that the government pays its employees annually is greater than the total amount that it spends on contractors annually

GO ON TO THE NEXT PAGE.

3. Biologist: DNA analysis shows that *Acacia heterophylla*, a tree native to the Indian Ocean's Réunion Island, is descended from the Hawaiian tree *Acacia koa*. Some think this occurred because *A. koa* seeds floated from Hawaii to Réunion, but that explanation is implausible, since the seeds will not germinate after being soaked in seawater. Moreover, both trees grow in the mountains, not near the shore. Seabirds sometimes carry seeds great distances, so they probably caused the dispersal.

Which one of the following, if true, most strengthens the support for the biologist's hypothesis?

(A) *A. koa* branches carrying seeds can remain afloat for prolonged periods of time.
(B) There are mountain-nesting seabird species common to Réunion and Hawaii.
(C) *A. koa* is thought to be descended from *Acacia melanoxylon*, a tree native to eastern Australia.
(D) Ocean currents have sometimes carried buoyant objects from Hawaii to Réunion.
(E) Many seabird species return to land very infrequently, and often do so only to breed.

4. Although smaller class sizes are popular with parents and teachers, the evidence shows that large scale reductions in class size lead to only slight improvements in student performance. Because school finances are limited, the cost-benefit test that any educational policy must pass is not "Does this policy have any positive effect?" but rather "Is there a more productive use of education dollars?" So public funds would in fact be better spent on efforts to recruit and retain better teachers.

Which one of the following is an assumption required by the argument?

(A) Reducing class size is an extremely expensive type of educational reform measure.
(B) Dollar for dollar, efforts to recruit and retain good teachers yield larger improvements in student performance than do reductions in class size.
(C) Because reducing class size is a popular policy, it is much easier to get public approval for that policy than for most other educational policies.
(D) Reducing class size is the most cost effective way to recruit and retain good teachers.
(E) In practice, it is difficult to identify what would be the most productive use of education dollars.

5. Seasonal allergy symptoms are the immune system's response to pollen in the air. When large amounts of pollen are inhaled, it can trigger an inflammatory response that causes allergy symptoms. While there are medicines that minimize those symptoms, a more effective—though often impractical—strategy is simply to stay indoors on dry, windy days during allergy season.

Which one of the following is most strongly supported by the information above?

(A) Medicines that minimize seasonal allergy symptoms prevent people from inhaling large amounts of pollen.
(B) Most types of pollen do not cause seasonal allergy symptoms.
(C) People who stay indoors on dry, windy days during allergy season are unlikely to inhale large amounts of pollen.
(D) People who take medicines that minimize seasonal allergy symptoms tend to stay indoors on dry, windy days during allergy season.
(E) People who experience seasonal allergy symptoms typically use air filters that remove pollen from the air in their homes.

6. Saturn's moon Enceladus has a rocky core and an icy surface. Between these two layers, there must be a lake of liquid water. The Cassini space probe was used to measure the density of matter composing Enceladus. These measurements revealed something denser than ice between the core and surface of Enceladus, and that could only be liquid water.

Which one of the following most accurately expresses the overall conclusion drawn in the argument?

(A) Saturn's moon Enceladus has a rocky core and an icy surface.
(B) There must be a lake of liquid water between the rocky core and the icy surface of Enceladus.
(C) The Cassini space probe was used to measure the density of Enceladus.
(D) Density measurements reveal something denser than ice between the core and surface of Enceladus.
(E) Anything denser than ice between the core and surface of Enceladus would have to be liquid water.

GO ON TO THE NEXT PAGE.

7. Thousands of fossils from the long-extinct dire wolf have been found in a cluster of natural tar pits in which animals became trapped and were preserved for millennia. None of these fossils came from dire wolf pups under six months old. Pups under six months old, therefore, probably did not accompany adults that were scavenging or hunting.

   Which one of the following is an assumption required by the argument?

   (A) Dire wolf pups under six months old would not have contributed to the adults' success in scavenging or hunting.
   (B) If a dire wolf pup under six months old became trapped in a tar pit, it would be better able to pull itself free than an adult dire wolf would.
   (C) Before the dire wolf became extinct, more dire wolves became trapped in the tar pits than did any other animal species.
   (D) The entrapment of dire wolves in the tar pits most frequently occurred when those animals were scavenging or hunting.
   (E) For the dire wolves that lived nearby, the tar pits were a favorite location for scavenging and hunting.

8. If a garden does not receive plenty of water and sunlight and is not planted in rich soil, then it will not be productive. Patricia has located her garden in an area that is ideal for receiving water and sunlight, and has made sure the soil is rich by adding fertilizer and compost. Hence, Patricia's garden will be productive.

   The reasoning in the argument is flawed in that the argument

   (A) fails to specify adequately the meaning in context of the term "ideal"
   (B) infers a cause from a correlation
   (C) confuses a cause with its effect
   (D) takes a set of necessary conditions as sufficient
   (E) relies on a sample that is unlikely to be representative

9. Rodents are small, gnawing mammals characterized by their chisel-like incisor teeth. Although most North American mammal species are not rodent species, most of the individual mammals in North America are rodents.

   Which one of the following is most strongly supported by the information above?

   (A) Most species of North American mammals have chisel-like incisor teeth.
   (B) In North America, rodent species tend to have more individual members than other species of mammals have.
   (C) Most species of mammals that have chisel-like incisor teeth can be found in North America.
   (D) Of the mammal species in North America, the one with the most individual members is a species of rodent.
   (E) Most nonrodent mammal species can be found in North America.

10. Toning shoes—walking shoes with a specially rounded sole—are popular with fitness enthusiasts. Research shows that the major leg muscles of people walking in toning shoes receive no more exercise than those of people walking in ordinary walking shoes. Nevertheless, many people experience a strengthening of their major leg muscles after switching to toning shoes.

    Which one of the following, if true, most helps to resolve the apparent discrepancy in the information above?

    (A) Toning shoes strengthen small underused muscles in the feet and ankles.
    (B) Muscles in the leg adapt to the rounded shape of toning shoes almost immediately.
    (C) Many people find toning shoes especially comfortable and walk more as a result.
    (D) There is little evidence that toning shoes cause injuries to their wearers.
    (E) Shoes that strengthen the major leg muscles are more marketable than ordinary shoes.

GO ON TO THE NEXT PAGE.

11. Psychologist: Specialists naturally tend to view their own specialties as fundamentally important. We are therefore amply justified in being skeptical when geneticists claim that personality traits not traditionally thought to be genetically determined are, in fact, genetically determined. The geneticists are probably just amplifying their sense of their own importance.

    The reasoning in the psychologist's argument is flawed in that this argument

    (A) generalizes about all specialists on the basis of an unrepresentative sample
    (B) presumes that the traditional view must be the right view simply because it is what has been traditionally believed
    (C) draws a conclusion that is merely a restatement of one of its main premises
    (D) appeals to the authority of those unlikely to be well informed about the topic at issue
    (E) disputes a claim on the basis of a supposed motive for making the claim rather than by assessing the evidence relevant to the claim

12. After the disastrous 1986 accident at the Chernobyl nuclear plant, the surrounding area was contaminated with radiation. Wild animals that are now there have very high levels of radiation in their muscles and bones. And yet since the disaster, wildlife populations in the region have expanded rapidly.

    Which one of the following, if true, most helps to resolve the apparent discrepancy in the information above?

    (A) Animals that did not arrive in the area around the Chernobyl nuclear plant until after the accident still developed high levels of radiation in their muscles and bones.
    (B) Some of the species that inhabit the region are migratory and so only live in the region for part of the year, limiting their exposure to the radiation.
    (C) The region affected by the release of radiation is very large, encompassing 1,800 square miles (4,660 square kilometers).
    (D) While some of the radioactive chemicals released by the accident depress fertility in local birds, others do not.
    (E) The threat of radiation poisoning drove people out of the area, which opened up new habitat for wildlife and eliminated the danger from hunters.

13. Commentator: The worldwide oil crisis of 1973 was not due to any real shortage of oil, but was the result of collusion between international oil companies and oil-producing countries to artificially restrict the supply of oil in order to profit from higher prices. This is shown by the fact that after 1973 the profits of oil companies showed large increases, as did the incomes of oil-producing countries.

    The reasoning in the commentator's argument is most vulnerable to criticism on the grounds that the argument

    (A) fails to consider the possibility that a party can benefit from an event without helping to bring about that event
    (B) presumes, without providing justification, that oil companies and oil-producing countries were the only parties to benefit from the 1973 oil crisis
    (C) rests on using the term "profit" in an ambiguous way
    (D) fails to establish that there was a worldwide oil surplus prior to the crisis of 1973
    (E) fails to consider the possibility that events that occur simultaneously can be causally related

14. In a study, six medical students were each separately presented with the same patient, whose symptoms could be the result of any one of several medical conditions. The attending physician asked each student a leading question of the form, "What tests should we order to try to rule out a diagnosis of X?" where X was filled in with a different medical condition for each student. A week later each student was presented with a patient having similar symptoms in the presence of a different attending physician who asked for a diagnosis without asking any leading questions. Each student began by testing the diagnosis that had been suggested by the original attending physician.

    Which one of the following statements is most strongly supported by the information above?

    (A) On the second occasion, none of the medical students began by testing the same diagnosis as any of the other medical students.
    (B) At most one of the medical students knew which of the several medical conditions was most likely to lead to the patients' symptoms.
    (C) The second attending physician was unaware of the results of the students' encounter with the first attending physician.
    (D) On the second occasion, exactly one of the students tested for the medical condition that actually caused the patient's symptoms.
    (E) At least some of the medical students were unaware that the patients' symptoms could be the result of medical conditions other than the one suggested by the original attending physician.

GO ON TO THE NEXT PAGE.

15. Few, if any, carbonated beverages contain calcium. Some very popular ones, however, contain significant amounts of caffeine, and consuming caffeine causes people to excrete significantly more calcium than they would otherwise. Interestingly, teenagers who drink large amounts of carbonated beverages containing caffeine tend to suffer more broken bones than those who do not. Calcium deficiency can make bones more brittle, of course, so the higher incidence of broken bones in teenagers who consume carbonated beverages with caffeine is probably due primarily to caffeine consumption.

    Which one of the following, if true, most weakens the argument?

    (A) Teenagers who drink large quantities of carbonated beverages containing caffeine tend to drink smaller quantities of calcium-rich beverages than other teenagers do.
    (B) Teenagers engage in the types of activities that carry a high risk of causing broken bones much more often than both older and younger people do.
    (C) Some teenagers have calcium deficiencies even though they do not consume any caffeine.
    (D) Some of the less popular carbonated beverages contain even more caffeine than the more popular ones.
    (E) The more calcium a person ingests as a regular part of his or her diet, the more calcium that person will tend to excrete.

16. Philosopher: Groups are not the type of entity that can be worthy of praise or blame. Blameworthiness implies conscience and agency. Nations do not have consciences. Families are not agents. Hence, any ascription of praise or blame to a group must be translated into some statement about individuals if we are to evaluate it properly.

    Which one of the following most accurately describes the role played in the philosopher's argument by the claim that nations do not have consciences?

    (A) It is an intermediate conclusion offered as direct support for the argument's main conclusion.
    (B) It is offered as support for an intermediate conclusion that is in turn offered as direct support for the argument's main conclusion.
    (C) It is cited as an implication of the main conclusion drawn in the argument.
    (D) It is cited as an instance of a general conclusion drawn in the argument.
    (E) It is the main conclusion drawn in the argument.

17. Psychiatrist: Psychological stress is known both to cause negative emotions and to impair physical health. This suggests that overcoming such negative emotions when they arise could cause one's health to improve.

    The psychiatrist's argument is most vulnerable to criticism on which one of the following grounds?

    (A) It presumes without justification that two conditions that together have a certain effect causally influence one another.
    (B) It presumes, merely on the basis that two conditions have a common cause, that one of these two conditions can causally influence the other.
    (C) It confuses two causes that together are necessary to bring about an effect with causes that are sufficient for that effect.
    (D) It takes for granted that two conditions that together have a certain effect can, each by itself, produce the same effect.
    (E) It takes for granted that removing a condition that causally contributes to another condition suffices to eliminate the latter condition.

18. Some potential anticancer drugs work by depriving growing tumors of needed blood vessels. The creation of blood vessels is called angiogenesis, and the experimental drugs work by inhibiting this process. The same drugs have been found to prevent obesity in rodents.

    The statements above, if true, lend the strongest support to which one of the following?

    (A) The cells in tumors are more similar in structure to fat cells than to other cells in the body.
    (B) Drugs that inhibit angiogenesis would probably enable obese humans to lose weight.
    (C) Fat tissue depends on angiogenesis in order to grow.
    (D) Rodents with cancer are more likely to be obese than healthy rodents.
    (E) Drugs that inhibit angiogenesis also prevent absorption of vital nutrients.

GO ON TO THE NEXT PAGE.

19. Although the slightest difference in shades of paint is noticeable, it is pointless to spend much time trying to match an old paint precisely when repainting only part of the interior of a house. This is because paint fades somewhat in the months after it has been applied. Thus, even if a new paint matches the old during application, the two paints will no longer match after a year or so.

The reasoning in which one of the following is most similar to that in the argument above?

(A) A bicycle is most comfortable to ride when the wheels are perfectly aligned. However, because the position of a bike wheel always shifts a bit when the bike is ridden, it is useless to put very much effort into perfectly aligning a new wheel.

(B) It is rarely worthwhile to look for parts for an older car. Because most cars do not last more than 20 years, it is best to buy a new car instead of restoring an older car.

(C) Keeping hair healthy requires using a shampoo designed specifically for one's hair type. However, hair will become unhealthy if washed consistently with the same brand of shampoo. Thus, to maintain healthy hair, a person should alternate between two suitable shampoos.

(D) Although cookies made with butter have a better texture than do cookies made with margarine, it is pointless to spend the extra money needed to buy butter, when cookies made with margarine are almost as good.

(E) Unless the size and shape of a dress exactly matches the size and shape of its lining, the dress will hang unevenly when it is worn. However, because most people would not notice this unevenness, it is not worthwhile when making a dress to spend much time attempting to match a dress and its lining perfectly.

20. Social observer: Advertising agencies are willfully neglecting the most profitable segment of the market: older adults. Older adults control more of this nation's personal disposable income than does the rest of the population combined. Therefore, advertising agencies can maximize their clients' profits if they gear their advertisements mainly to older adults.

Which one of the following, if assumed, would enable the conclusion of the social observer's argument to be properly inferred?

(A) Older people generally have larger incomes and have had longer to accumulate resources than younger people.

(B) No company can maximize its profits unless it markets its products primarily to a population segment that controls most of this nation's personal disposable income.

(C) Advertising that is directed toward the wealthiest people is the most effective means for a business to improve the reputation of its products.

(D) No advertising agency that tailors its advertisements mainly to an audience that does not control much of this nation's personal disposable income will maximize its clients' profits.

(E) Any advertising agency that gears its advertisements mainly to a population segment that controls 50 percent or more of this nation's personal disposable income will maximize its clients' profits.

GO ON TO THE NEXT PAGE.

21. Professor: It has been argued that all judges should be elected rather than appointed to their positions. But this is a bad idea. If judges ran for election, they would have to raise campaign funds. Thus, they would be likely to accept campaign contributions from special interests. It is well-known that such contributions lead to conflicts of interest for politicians, so it is to be expected that they would produce similar conflicts of interest for judges.

Which one of the following principles, if valid, would most help to justify the professor's reasoning?

(A) If politicians should avoid conflicts of interest, then judges should avoid conflicts of interest as well.
(B) Special interests should not make offers of campaign contributions to those running for elective office.
(C) Judges should be appointed to their positions only if doing so ensures that they will usually be able to avoid conflicts of interest.
(D) If judges should be appointed, then it is likely that there are other public offices that should be changed from elected to appointed offices.
(E) No public office for which election campaigning would be likely to produce conflicts of interest should be changed from an appointed to an elected office.

22. Merle: Usually when I insert a dollar bill into the change machine at the office it makes a squeaking sound before it produces change. But the machine can make the sound only when the electric outlet it is plugged into is turned on. Therefore, it must be that the electric outlet usually is turned on.

Which one of the following arguments exhibits flawed reasoning most similar to the flawed reasoning exhibited by Merle's argument?

(A) Everyone who has read the new horror novel found the plot disturbing. Indeed, the plot would disturb anyone with a vivid imagination. Therefore, everyone who has read the novel must have a vivid imagination.
(B) Some people who have read the new horror novel found the plot disturbing. But the plot would not be disturbing to people who lack vivid imaginations. Therefore, some people must have vivid imaginations.
(C) Many people who have read the new horror novel found the plot disturbing. Undoubtedly, everyone who found the plot disturbing has a vivid imagination. Therefore, many of the people who have read the novel must have vivid imaginations.
(D) Most people who have read the new horror novel found the plot disturbing. But the plot cannot disturb anyone who lacks a vivid imagination. Therefore, most people must have vivid imaginations.
(E) Most people who have read the new horror novel found the plot disturbing. But the plot cannot disturb people who lack vivid imaginations. Therefore, most people with vivid imaginations must find the plot disturbing.

23. Kira: It would be unwise for you to buy that insurance policy. It's designed to make money for the company that sells it to you. They set the prices to ensure profits.

Binh: Undeniably, the insurer is in business to make money. But the mere fact that an insurer draws a profit in no way implies that buying one of its policies is unwise.

Binh responds to Kira's argument by doing which one of the following?

(A) suggesting that Kira has overlooked a fact that, although consistent with her premises, is in direct conflict with her conclusion
(B) denying Kira's premises while suggesting that her conclusion, although possibly true, is highly unlikely
(C) arguing that Kira's premises are not only inadequate to prove her conclusion but in fact point strongly toward its being false
(D) conceding Kira's premises without denying her conclusion, while asserting that the latter does not follow from the former
(E) observing that while Kira's premises each independently support her conclusion, the premises themselves are inconsistent with one another

24. Economist: The increase in the minimum wage in Country X will quickly lead to a decrease in Country X's rate of unemployment. Raising the minimum wage will lead to more disposable income for a large segment of the working population. Much of this increased income will be spent on consumer goods. Surely this increase in demand for consumer goods will lead to an increase in the number of factory jobs necessary to meet production.

Each of the following, if true, would weaken the economist's argument EXCEPT:

(A) The cost of a minimum-wage increase in Country X will be passed on to consumers in the form of significantly higher prices for consumer goods.
(B) Most of the consumer goods sold in Country X are produced outside the country.
(C) In many factories in Country X, most workers are paid much more than the current minimum wage.
(D) The cost to employers of an increase in the minimum wage in Country X will be made up by reductions in the workforce.
(E) Most factories that produce consumer goods in Country X have large surpluses of goods as a result of years of overproduction.

GO ON TO THE NEXT PAGE.

25. Art critic: An arrangement of objects tends to be aesthetically pleasing to the extent that it gives the impression that the person who arranged the objects succeeded at what he or she was attempting to do.

The generalization expressed by the art critic, if correct, most helps to justify the reasoning in which one of the following arguments?

(A) The new art installation is very pleasing aesthetically. However, even though it is not apparent to viewers, the artist did not intend the wooden panels to be arranged the way they in fact are. So the panels should be rearranged to reflect the artist's intention.

(B) The wooden panels in the art installation probably are not arranged in the way that the artist wanted them arranged, for the installation is less aesthetically pleasing than other installations.

(C) The arrangement of wooden panels in the art installation is likely to give the impression that the artist who arranged them did not quite succeed at what she was attempting to do, for the arrangement is almost, but not quite, symmetrical.

(D) The art installation would be more aesthetically pleasing if the wooden panels in it were arranged more symmetrically, for then it would seem more like the artist had gotten the panels arranged the way she wanted.

(E) The artist could make the arrangement of wooden panels in the art installation more aesthetically pleasing by making it less symmetrical, for then it would give less of an impression that every aspect of the arrangement was fully planned.

26. The three-spine stickleback is a small fish that lives both in oceans and in freshwater lakes. While ocean stickleback are covered with armor to protect them from their predators, lake stickleback have virtually no armor. Since armor limits the speed of a stickleback's growth, this indicates that having a larger size is a better defense against the lake stickleback's predators than having armor.

Which one of the following, if true, weakens the argument?

(A) Sticklebacks with armor are unable to swim as fast, making them most vulnerable to fast-moving predators.

(B) Having a larger size is an important factor in whether lake stickleback, but not ocean stickleback, survive cold winters.

(C) Unlike ocean stickleback, the lake stickleback are more often preyed upon by predatory insects than by larger fish.

(D) Both ocean stickleback and lake stickleback feed primarily on the same types of foods.

(E) Sticklebacks originated in the ocean but began populating freshwater lakes and streams following the last ice age.

S T O P

IF YOU FINISH BEFORE TIME IS CALLED, YOU MAY CHECK YOUR WORK ON THIS SECTION ONLY.
DO NOT WORK ON ANY OTHER SECTION IN THE TEST.

SECTION III
Time—35 minutes
27 Questions

Directions: Each set of questions in this section is based on a single passage or a pair of passages. The questions are to be answered on the basis of what is stated or implied in the passage or pair of passages. For some questions, more than one of the choices could conceivably answer the question. However, you are to choose the best answer; that is, choose the response that most accurately and completely answers the question and mark that response on your answer sheet.

The following passage is adapted from a 2001 article by a film historian.

In exhibiting works of art—whether in a gallery, a cinema, or anywhere else—the primary question usually is: which works should be exhibited together? In many exhibitions the selection is often tied to the
(5) creator of the works. For example, we might have an exhibition of Rembrandt's paintings. Another reasonable method might be to choose paintings with a particular theme or of a particular historical period, for example, Modernism. In all cases the aim is to select a
(10) series of works with something in common. In the world of cinema, this notion of "collecting the similar" has its analogue in the retrospective. This involves collecting together and screening several examples of the work of a particular director, star, studio, etc. In
(15) recent years a rediscovery of early (pre-1915) nonfiction film has been taking place, and such films have been the subject of some notable retrospectives.

But I would argue that the philosophy of "collecting the similar" is often inappropriate for
(20) screening early film, especially nonfiction, because it means showing several films of the same type one after the other in the same sitting, which would never have been the practice at the time the films were made. Gathering together several short films (and in the early
(25) 1910s most films were under fifteen minutes) by the same maker or studio, while useful for historians and academics, is often profoundly dull for the viewer. With some exceptions, nonfiction films have always been supporting films, not main attractions. Early
(30) cinemagoers never saw a collection of similar films screened together; they almost always saw a program that was a mix of everything from dramas and comedies to travelogues and news. Even into the 1920s a mixed program was the norm.

(35) Film archives and retrospective festivals often behave as if the production of the films were the only side of the coin. Film archives spend vast amounts of time and effort in restoring films as they supposedly were when originally produced. These restorations are
(40) presented with great fanfare as authentic versions, or "directors' cuts." Yet as far as the exhibition side is concerned, authenticity is sometimes allowed to go out the window. Films are presented in an inauthentic setting, utterly shorn of the program that once gave
(45) these films life and context, a setting that allowed particular films to shine, but also to balance and react against other kinds of films. Film presenters discovered the magic of programming in the early years of the twentieth century, or more likely inherited it from the
(50) vaudeville tradition. It ill behooves us alleged early film lovers to forsake their insights today.

1. Which one of the following most accurately expresses the main point of the passage?

    (A) Screenings that consist entirely of early nonfiction films are poorly conceived because they ignore the context of the films' original screening.
    (B) The practices that are best suited to exhibiting works in an artistic medium like painting are not well suited for exhibiting cinematic works.
    (C) Early nonfiction films have not received the critical recognition that they deserve.
    (D) The artistic goals of early nonfiction films are different in many major respects from the goals of contemporary cinema.
    (E) For modern audiences to properly experience early nonfiction films, film archivists must produce restorations of those films that are as authentic as possible.

2. According to the passage, which one of the following is true of early nonfiction films?

    (A) They were produced by studios that focused exclusively on nonfiction films.
    (B) They were rarely credited to individual directors.
    (C) They were heavily influenced by the vaudeville tradition.
    (D) They were usually intended to be supporting films.
    (E) They were no less popular than most comedies and dramas of the time.

GO ON TO THE NEXT PAGE.

3. The author would be most likely to reject which one of the following principles?

(A) Works of art should be presented as authentically as possible.
(B) Dissimilar works of art should never be displayed together.
(C) Contemporary exhibitions of works of art should be informed by knowledge of how past exhibitions collected works together.
(D) Art exhibitions should never be designed without regard to how each work contributes to the whole.
(E) Art exhibitions should sometimes collect works that are all by the same artist.

4. The passage contains information sufficient to answer which one of the following questions?

(A) How many nonfiction films were made in the years before 1915?
(B) Did directors of early nonfiction films ever work on other films as well?
(C) How long were most films in the early years of the twentieth century?
(D) Out of what historical tradition did the idea of "directors' cuts" originate?
(E) How popular were early travelogues and news films with audiences of their time?

5. The author most likely intends the final sentence of the passage to

(A) call into question the sincerity of those who purport to be early film aficionados
(B) carry an implication regarding the proper way of exhibiting early nonfiction films
(C) trace the historical basis behind the screening practices of early twentieth century film presenters
(D) suggest that it is incumbent upon those who enjoy early films to seek out the earliest versions they can find
(E) challenge the notion that early film can ever be fully understood by contemporary audiences

6. The author would be most likely to agree with which one of the following statements?

(A) An exhibition of works by a single artist is likely to be less interesting than an exhibition that contains a mixture of works by different artists.
(B) When several works of art are exhibited together, the audience's response can be greatly affected by the interplay among those works.
(C) Film archives and retrospective festivals are too beholden to practices that have their roots in the vaudeville tradition.
(D) Most early cinemagoers did not think of nonfiction films of the time as belonging to a separate genre from comedies and dramas.
(E) A work of art will be misunderstood by historians or academics unless it is viewed in an authentic setting.

7. It can be inferred from the passage that the author holds which one of the following views regarding the "directors' cuts" described in the final paragraph?

(A) They are usually little more than clever marketing gimmicks and are entirely lacking in artistic value.
(B) Producing them is largely a pointless endeavor, in that it is striving for a goal that can never be fully achieved.
(C) Paradoxically, even though they are produced in an attempt to increase authenticity, in many cases they are less authentic than other versions.
(D) The time and effort expended in producing them is potentially wasted if no attention is paid to other aspects of authenticity.
(E) In the vast majority of cases where such a version is available, it represents by far the best way to experience the film.

GO ON TO THE NEXT PAGE.

With rapidly expanding populations, growing industrial development, and dwindling water supplies on national and regional levels, water is fast replacing oil as the world's most valuable resource. Meanwhile, (5) the growing importance of water in geopolitical affairs has increased the potential for international conflict over water resources. Thus as development and other threats to the world's rivers have continued to mount, nations have become acutely aware of the need (10) for legal and institutional mechanisms to manage and protect resources that traverse their borders. Recognition of the need for international cooperation in efforts to manage and protect rivers has led the United Nations' International Law Commission (ILC) (15) to develop a treaty structure for the uses of international watercourses.

The ILC's *Draft Articles* on the Law of the Non-Navigational Uses of International Watercourses are an attempt to codify the customary principles of (20) international water law as those principles are manifested in past legal decisions and currently accepted international practice. The *Draft Articles* are intended as a set of guidelines for the creation of treaties governing the use of specific international (25) watercourses. They prescribe that treaties should uphold several broad precepts: that one nation's use of a watercourse should not cause appreciable harm to another nation, that every nation's use of the watercourse should be equitable and reasonable, and (30) that nations should work for the protection of ecosystems.

Though the *Draft Articles* are a significant step forward in the formulation of legal principles for the protection and regulation of international rivers, they (35) are inadequate because they do not provide satisfactory ways of dealing with possible future environmental changes. One significant environmental threat to the world's rivers is the increase of atmospheric carbon dioxide. With its resultant greenhouse effect and (40) warmer temperatures, it is likely to have a number of dramatic effects on water levels in international river systems, arising from increased runoff due to snowmelt or, more importantly, from decreased precipitation in many regions.

(45) Treaties that allocate fixed amounts of water to various countries based on current usage, as suggested by the *Draft Articles*, will not be flexible enough to respond to these large fluctuations in river flows. Once specific water rights are allocated along a river in (50) accordance with the *Draft Articles*, nations would have no mechanism for coping with a drastic reduction in the flow of the river. Adhering rigidly to these fixed allocations would unjustly favor those countries whose water usage is most extensive. One way to circumvent (55) this problem is to devise treaties that apportion water use in more flexible ways—for example, by assigning proportional shares rather than fixed allotments of water. Similarly, treaties might incorporate explicit contingency plans dealing specifically with issues (60) related to possible climate changes, such as how reduced flows will be allocated among the countries sharing a river.

8. Which one of the following most accurately expresses the main point of the passage?

(A) The world's water resources are on the decline, so the ILC has formulated a set of treaty guidelines designed to ensure each nation's equitable use of watercourses, protect ecosystems, and prevent one country's use of a watercourse from harming another country.

(B) The potential for international conflict over dwindling water resources is escalating due to climatic changes, so the ILC has developed a treaty structure in an effort to ensure and safeguard the continued growth of industrial development on national and regional levels.

(C) Though the ILC's *Draft Articles* are a worthwhile attempt to assemble an appropriate set of principles to govern the formulation of treaties concerning the use of international watercourses, they are flawed because of their lack of provision for the foreseeable effects of certain predicted environmental changes.

(D) While the environmental threats to the world's water resources have thus far had little impact on river systems, the ILC's *Draft Articles* can and should be suitably revised to take into account possible future threats that could significantly alter the world's rivers.

(E) The increase in atmospheric carbon dioxide and the attendant greenhouse effect and resultant global warming have already had detrimental effects on international river systems, and the ILC's *Draft Articles* fail to outline adequate contingency plans to deal with these environmental changes.

9. Which one of the following is proposed by the author as a way for countries to respond to the danger that serious water-usage problems may result from changes in the flow of international rivers?

(A) regulating industrial development in countries with rapidly expanding economies
(B) developing mechanisms to sustain and safeguard the balance of ecosystems
(C) allocating water usage amounts to countries based on a proportional share system
(D) modifying agricultural practices that require inordinate amounts of water
(E) redirecting snowmelt runoff to areas with increased water needs

GO ON TO THE NEXT PAGE.

10. According to the passage, a primary purpose for the development of the *Draft Articles* was to

    (A) criticize existing international practices resulting from past legal decisions
    (B) provide an explicit formulation of some commonly applied principles of international law
    (C) establish uniform judicial procedures for deciding disputes over water resources
    (D) protect the pre-existing water rights of those countries that use the most water
    (E) help guarantee continued industrial development in countries that share rivers

11. In the passage, the author claims that the *Draft Articles* are flawed in that they

    (A) focus on the management of water resources rather than on the protection of rivers endangered by environmental changes
    (B) fail to incorporate certain widely accepted legal principles reflected in customary international water-use practices
    (C) do not address pertinent issues involving the relationship between navigational and non-navigational uses of international watercourses
    (D) suggest that treaties stipulate specific quantities of water use, which future conditions may render inequitable
    (E) provide little assistance to countries in the process of expanding their water uses, and thus favor more industrialized countries

12. The passage most strongly supports the inference that the author would agree with which one of the following statements?

    (A) It is possible to devise treaties that uphold the broad precepts embraced in the *Draft Articles* and that also permit countries to adapt to large fluctuations in river flows.
    (B) Efforts to manage and protect the world's water resources should include unilateral regulatory action on the part of the ILC in cases where treaties do not adequately provide for the protection of internationally shared watercourses.
    (C) The *Draft Articles* need to be reformulated to take into account the effects of water usage on entire river systems instead of focusing on the individual segments of such systems that lie entirely within each nation's borders.
    (D) Many existing treaties governing water usage are cast in terms that permit nations to react flexibly to altered water availability patterns that might occur due to global warming.
    (E) Countries that use the greatest quantities of water have generally favored treaties formulated in terms that allocate fixed quantities of water usage to each participating country.

13. The passage most strongly suggests that which one of the following was true at the time the ILC began developing the *Draft Articles*?

    (A) Water resources were sufficiently abundant to meet the needs of most of the countries belonging to the United Nations.
    (B) Precipitation levels throughout the world had been declining steadily for a number of years.
    (C) Existing treaties governing water rights rarely covered matters involving environmental protection.
    (D) Conflicts over the management of water resources had been escalating sharply in frequency and intensity.
    (E) Much of the content of the *Draft Articles* had already been articulated by courts resolving international water-rights cases.

14. Which one of the following most accurately characterizes the author's attitude toward the *Draft Articles*?

    (A) mistrust of the political motivations that shaped them
    (B) skepticism regarding their assumption that treaties are the only viable type of water-usage agreement
    (C) concern over their failure to prescribe ways of dealing with treaty violations
    (D) satisfaction with their initiative in diverging from international customary practice
    (E) approval of the general goals that they attempt to accomplish

15. The author probably intends the phrase "treaty structure" in the last sentence of the first paragraph to refer to

    (A) an outline for a comprehensive international accord intended to serve in place of individual bilateral treaties between countries
    (B) a compendium of past treaties that the ILC regards as exemplary models for the formulation of future treaties
    (C) a systematic analysis of legal precedents that have been established by international tribunals in adjudicating treaty-related disputes
    (D) a set of general prescriptive principles to be followed in the formulation of the provisions of treaties
    (E) a charter for a proposed advisory board that would oversee treaty negotiation on behalf of the international community

GO ON TO THE NEXT PAGE.

This passage was adapted from an article published in 2000.

Competition to make computer chips smaller and, consequently, faster and more efficient has driven a technological revolution, fueled economic growth, and rapidly made successive generations of computers
(5) obsolete. Yet at the current rate of progress this march toward miniaturization will hit a wall by about 2010—for many, an unthinkable prospect. The laws of physics dictate that, with current methods, properly functioning transistors—the electronic devices that make up
(10) computer chips—cannot be made smaller than 25 nanometers (billionths of a meter). In living cells, however, natural chemical processes efficiently and precisely produce extremely complex structures below this size limit, so there may be hope of using some such
(15) processes to yield tiny molecules that can either function like transistors or be induced to combine with other materials in carefully controlled ways to construct whole nanocircuits. Much current research is aimed at harnessing DNA to this end, but materials chemist
(20) Angela Belcher and physicist Evelyn Hu are investigating a different molecular pattern maker: peptides, amino acid chains that are shorter than proteins.

The project grew out of Belcher's doctoral
(25) research on abalone. Her research group discovered in the mid-1990s that a specific peptide causes calcium carbonate to crystallize into the structure found only in the tough abalone shell. From that discovery, Belcher and Hu, Belcher's postdoctoral adviser at the time,
(30) realized that if they found peptides able to direct the crystal growth of the semiconductor materials that form transistors, they might have a tool for building nanoscale electronics. However, no known peptide was able to bind to semiconductor materials to cause the
(35) development of particular crystalline structures as some peptides did with calcium carbonate. So Belcher, Hu, and their colleagues grew a random assortment of one billion different peptides and tested whether any of them bound to silicon, gallium arsenide, or indium
(40) phosphide crystals—three widely used semiconductor materials. They found a few peptides that not only bound exclusively to one of the crystals in the experiment but also latched onto a particular face of the crystal. Through a process resembling accelerated
(45) evolution, they developed additional related peptides from those that had the initially promising characteristics.

Hu says that in order to use such a method to assemble a set of circuit-building tools it would be
(50) necessary to identify many additional organic compounds that bind to circuit-component materials. The group is making progress on that quest. As they have expanded their targets to 20 more semiconductor materials, their cache of crystal-manipulating peptides
(55) has ballooned into the hundreds. They are also designing new peptides that bind to two different crystals at once, acting as a daub of glue. It will take that kind of finesse at the nanoscale to produce self-assembling circuits.

16. Which one of the following most accurately expresses the main point of the passage?

(A) Although preliminary results suggest that Belcher and Hu's research on peptides and semiconductors could result in a breakthrough in the miniaturization of computer chips, enough obstacles remain to make such an outcome unlikely.
(B) Advances in computer chip speed and efficiency beyond the year 2010 may depend on the outcome of various current research projects, including that conducted by Belcher and Hu, which focus on using peptides to bind different crystals together.
(C) Belcher and Hu's research on the abilities of some peptides to bind to semiconductor materials indicates that peptides might eventually be applied to the production of computer chips with transistors smaller than the lower limit set by current methods.
(D) Belcher and Hu's discovery of peptides that cause the development of a particular crystalline structure in a natural biological context suggests that semiconductor materials might bind to biological compounds.
(E) The application of Belcher's work on abalone to the world of semiconductors shows that pure scientific research can have unexpected practical repercussions.

17. The words "that kind of finesse" (final sentence of the passage) refer primarily to

(A) the ability to translate abstract, theoretical concepts in computer design into concrete applications
(B) the creativity that was necessary to apply knowledge gained from DNA research to molecular pattern makers other than DNA
(C) the development of sophisticated methods of observing the behavior of crystalline structures that are both extremely tiny and extremely complex
(D) the ability to differentiate peptides that interact chemically with at least one semiconductor material from very similar peptides that do not interact with any such materials
(E) the ability of researchers to manipulate organic compounds in ways that satisfy very specific circuit-construction needs

GO ON TO THE NEXT PAGE.

18. Which one of the following statements about the peptides that Belcher and Hu tested in relation to semiconductors can be most reasonably inferred from the passage?

    (A) At least some of them did not previously exist in nature.
    (B) At least one of them was found to bind to three different semiconductor compounds.
    (C) At least some of them were tested in relation to silicon but not in relation to gallium arsenide.
    (D) At least one of them was in use in the computer chip industry prior to Belcher and Hu's research.
    (E) Other researchers had previously tested at least some of them for possible reactions with semiconductor materials other than silicon, gallium arsenide, and indium phosphide.

19. Which one of the following situations involving volatile oils is most analogous to the situation involving peptides that is presented in the passage?

    (A) A group of researchers, whose experimentation has focused on the chemical properties of certain synthetic volatile oils, abandons that line of inquiry on receiving a grant to study whether certain species of trees contain acids that could have antiviral properties in human medical applications.
    (B) A group of researchers extracts several volatile oils from the leaves of certain species of trees and, while testing each of the oils to determine whether it has antifungal properties that could make it useful in human medical applications, they discover that one of the oils is a powerful insecticide.
    (C) A group of researchers synthesizes several volatile oils that, when combined, are found to be useful as a fungicide on fruit trees. Through further experimentation, they find that this same combination of oils has antiviral properties in human medical applications.
    (D) A group of researchers observes that a volatile oil contained in an antifungal product used on fruit trees can cause mutations in the trees. As a result, they launch a research project to determine whether similar oils that are used in human medical applications might cause genetic damage.
    (E) A group of researchers, noting that a volatile oil secreted by a certain species of tree protects it from a type of fungal infection, synthesizes several similar oils and tests them for possible antibacterial activity that might make them useful in human medical applications.

20. The primary role of the first two sentences of the passage is to help the reader understand

    (A) why research of the sort done by Belcher and Hu was not previously undertaken by other researchers
    (B) the purpose and importance of the research that Belcher and Hu have undertaken
    (C) the skepticism with which some members of the scientific community have greeted Belcher and Hu's research
    (D) a commonly held viewpoint against which Belcher and Hu's research is directed
    (E) a hypothesis that Belcher and Hu's research is designed to test

21. The passage most strongly supports which one of the following?

    (A) Some peptides that bind to gallium arsenide also bind to indium phosphide.
    (B) Researchers besides Belcher and Hu and their colleagues have studied the possibility of using peptides in the assembly of nanocircuits.
    (C) Neither Belcher nor Hu has done major scientific research on organic compounds other than peptides.
    (D) Silicon, gallium arsenide, and indium phosphide are not the only semiconductor materials to which peptides have been found to bind.
    (E) Peptides have been used in industrial applications that are not related to semiconductors.

22. Which one of the following, if true, lends the most support to a prediction of an eventual commercial application of Belcher and Hu's research into peptides and semiconductors?

    (A) Belcher and Hu's early successes in synthesizing peptides that bind to semiconductors have sparked renewed interest in possible DNA applications in the construction of nanocircuits.
    (B) For almost any semiconductor material that is used in a computer circuit, there are many other semiconductor materials that function in the same way and could be substituted for it.
    (C) The number of peptides that bind to two different crystals at once appears to be smaller than the number of peptides that, although they bind to two different crystals, cannot bind to both at the same time.
    (D) The one billion peptides that Belcher and Hu grew and tested in the initial stages of their research was nearly four times the number of peptides they grew and tested subsequently.
    (E) Expectations of continuing high costs of synthesizing the peptides that Belcher and Hu have found to bind to semiconductors have tended to restrict the number of scientists contemplating possible research into peptide uses in nanocircuits.

GO ON TO THE NEXT PAGE.

Passage A

In 1940, Benjamin Lee Whorf seduced a whole generation into believing that our mother tongue restricts what we are able to think. In particular, Whorf announced, Hopi and English impose different pictures
(5) of reality on their speakers, impeding mutual understanding. Eventually, it transpired that there had never actually been any evidence to support his fantastic claims.

Whorf's main mistake was to assume that our
(10) mother tongue prevents us from being able to think certain thoughts; new research suggests that in reality its influence consists in what it obliges us to think about. German, for example, forces me to designate my neighbor as male (*Nachbar*) or female (*Nachbarin*).
(15) Furthermore, grammatical genders can shape the feelings and associations that speakers have toward objects around them. In the 1990s, psychologists compared associations that speakers of German and Spanish make. There are many inanimate nouns whose
(20) genders in the two languages are reversed. A German bridge is feminine (*die Brücke*), for instance, but *el puente* is masculine in Spanish; and the same goes for clocks and violins. When speakers were asked about the characteristics of various objects, Spanish
(25) speakers deemed bridges, clocks, and violins to have stereotypically masculine properties like strength, but Germans tended to think of them as more slender or elegant. With objects like mountains or chairs, which are "he" in German but "she" in Spanish, the effect was
(30) reversed.

Passage B

Studies involving Pirahã and Mundurukú Indian subjects from the Brazilian Amazonia give evidence regarding the role of language in the development of numerical reasoning. The subjects in these reports
(35) apparently have consistent, unambiguous words for one and two and more loosely used words for three and four, but these subjects may not have true number words at all. Moreover, they do not overtly count, either with number words or by means of tallies. Yet, when
(40) tested on a variety of numerical tasks—naming the number of items in a stimulus set, constructing sets of equivalent number, judging which of two sets is more numerous, and mental addition and subtraction—the results appear to indicate that the subjects possess an
(45) innate imprecise nonverbal concept of number.

In showing that subjects with no verbal counting system have a concept of approximate numerical magnitude comparable to that of numerate subjects, these reports support a non-Whorfian, language-
(50) independent view of the origins of our concept of number. However, there is more to the story. Numerate subjects have a strong intuition of exact numerical equality. Two plus two is exactly four, not roughly four. When the innumerate subjects in these reports matched
(55) a set of four items to a set of five, or judged that 6–3=2, they gave evidence of being indifferent to exact numerical equality, an indifference not seen in numerate control subjects. Thus, the reports suggest that learning number words either creates a concept of exact
(60) numerical equality (a strong Whorfian hypothesis), or mediates the expansion of such a concept (a weaker Whorfian hypothesis), or directs attention to such a concept (a non-Whorfian hypothesis).

23. Both passages are concerned with answering which one of the following questions?

    (A) Are there limits to the translatability of one language into another?
    (B) What does scientific research reveal about the relation between language and thought?
    (C) Do differences among languages result from different ways of thinking about the world?
    (D) Were Whorf's claims about language based on better evidence than previously thought?
    (E) Is the influence of language on thought confined to specific areas such as number and gender?

24. In the first sentence of passage B, the word "subjects" refers to which one of the following?

    (A) words
    (B) topics
    (C) people
    (D) relations
    (E) objects

25. Which one of the following is true about the relationship between the two passages?

    (A) Passage A presents examples of languages that picture reality in compatible ways, whereas passage B presents examples of languages that picture reality in incompatible ways.
    (B) Passage A depicts language as influencing thought by means of its vocabulary, whereas passage B depicts language as influencing thought by means of its grammatical structure.
    (C) Passage A regards linguistic differences as rendering mutual understanding impossible, whereas passage B regards them as a surmountable obstacle to mutual understanding.
    (D) Passage A portrays linguistic differences as arising from conceptual differences, whereas passage B portrays conceptual differences as arising from linguistic differences.
    (E) Passage A focuses on differences in people's subjective associations, whereas passage B focuses on the possession of concepts.

GO ON TO THE NEXT PAGE.

26. Given the style and tone of each passage, which one of the following is most likely to be true?

    (A) The author of passage A is writing for a general audience, while the author of passage B is addressing a more academic audience.
    (B) The author of passage A is an anthropologist, while the author of passage B is a linguist.
    (C) The author of passage A is a neutral observer, while the author of passage B is an advocate of a particular view.
    (D) The author of passage A is interested mainly in the historical development of an idea, whereas the author of passage B is concerned with its truth.
    (E) The author of passage A is dismissive of the ideas under discussion, while the author of passage B takes them more seriously.

27. Which one of the following principles underlies the argument in passage B, but not that in passage A?

    (A) If different languages apply incompatible concepts to one and the same object, then that suggests those concepts were created by those languages.
    (B) If a speaker possesses a concept for which the speaker's language lacks an expression, then that suggests that the concept was not created by language.
    (C) If one's language prevented one from possessing certain concepts, then one would not be able to learn a language in which such concepts are represented.
    (D) If a concept can be expressed more exactly in one language than in another language, then it is likely that the concept was created by those languages.
    (E) If a language obliges speakers to think about a concept, that concept must have been obtained independently of the language.

STOP

IF YOU FINISH BEFORE TIME IS CALLED, YOU MAY CHECK YOUR WORK ON THIS SECTION ONLY.
DO NOT WORK ON ANY OTHER SECTION IN THE TEST.

SECTION IV
Time—35 minutes
25 Questions

Directions: Each question in this section is based on the reasoning presented in a brief passage. In answering the questions, you should not make assumptions that are by commonsense standards implausible, superfluous, or incompatible with the passage. For some questions, more than one of the choices could conceivably answer the question. However, you are to choose the best answer; that is, choose the response that most accurately and completely answers the question and mark that response on your answer sheet.

1. A company produced a small car that costs much less— but is also much less safe—than any car previously available. However, most customers of the new car increased their safety on the roads by buying it.

    Which one of the following, if true, most helps to resolve the apparent paradox in the above claims?

    (A) The company surveyed potential customers and discovered that most of them were more concerned about cost than about safety.
    (B) The company could significantly increase the car's safety without dramatically increasing its production cost.
    (C) Most people who bought the new car were probably unaware that it is much less safe than other cars.
    (D) Many households that previously could afford only one car can now afford two.
    (E) Most people who bought the new car previously travelled by bicycle or motorcycle, which are less safe than the new car.

2. Brian: I used to eat cheeseburgers from fast-food restaurants almost every day. But then I read that eating bread and meat in the same meal interferes with digestion. So I stopped eating cheeseburgers and switched to a diet of lean meats, fruits, and vegetables. Since starting this new diet, I feel much better and my cholesterol level and blood pressure are lower. This proves that eating bread and meat in the same meal is unhealthy.

    The reasoning in Brian's argument is flawed in that the argument

    (A) treats a statement as established fact merely because a self-appointed expert has asserted it
    (B) draws a conclusion that merely restates a premise offered in support of it
    (C) treats a condition that must occur in order for an effect to occur as a condition that would ensure that the effect occurs
    (D) concludes that one part of a change was responsible for an effect without ruling out the possibility that other parts of that change were responsible
    (E) concludes that making a dietary change improved the health of a particular person simply because that change results in improved health for most people

3. Researcher: Newly formed neurons can help to heal an injured brain but only if they develop into the type of neurons that are most common in the injured area. Studies have shown that when a part of the brain called the striatum is injured, newly formed neurons in the striatum never become midsized spiny neurons, the type most common in the striatum.

    If the researcher's statements are true, which one of the following must also be true?

    (A) Newly formed neurons sometimes develop into midsized spiny neurons in areas of the brain other than the striatum.
    (B) Newly formed neurons are commonly found in injured areas of the brain shortly after the injury occurs.
    (C) Midsized spiny neurons are not the most common type of neuron in any part of the brain other than the striatum.
    (D) In cases of injury to the striatum, newly formed neurons will not help to heal the injury.
    (E) In most cases of brain injury, newly formed neurons do not help to heal the injury.

GO ON TO THE NEXT PAGE.

4. Leona: Thompson's article on the novel *Emily's Trials* is intriguing but ultimately puzzling. In discussing one scene, Thompson says that a character's "furrowed brow" and grim expression indicate deep inner turmoil and anxiety. Later, however, Thompson refers to the same scene and describes this character as the "self-identified agent" of an action. This ascription is interesting and challenging in its own right; but Thompson begins the article by claiming that a "self-identified agent" is fundamentally incapable of having misgivings or anxiety.

The argumentative strategy Leona uses in discussing the article is to criticize Thompson's comments on the grounds that

(A) some of Thompson's reasoning is circular
(B) Thompson provides no definition of the concept of a "self-identified agent"
(C) the analysis of character offered by Thompson is insufficiently supported by the textual evidence
(D) it is unlikely that any character could qualify as a "self-identified agent"
(E) some of Thompson's claims contradict each other

5. An online auction site conducted a study of auction techniques involving 8,000 used cars, divided into two equal groups. Each car's listing in the first group included a brief description of its condition. The description of each car in the other half additionally listed defects of the car. More cars in the second group sold, and of comparable cars in both groups that sold, the cars in the second group fetched higher prices.

Which one of the following, if true, most helps to explain why the second group of cars had better sales results than the first group?

(A) Most people are skeptical of the descriptions that accompany items when they are put up for auction online.
(B) People are likely to assume that a car with no reported defects has been maintained more attentively and is therefore in better overall condition.
(C) Prospective buyers are likely to overlook mention of defects buried in a detailed description of the condition of an object they are considering purchasing.
(D) Listing defects in a description of an item tends to lead people to assume that no major defect has gone unmentioned.
(E) With thousands of cars for sale, prospective buyers are unlikely to read detailed descriptions of more than a small fraction of them.

6. Critic: Linsey has been judged to be a bad songwriter simply because her lyrics typically are disjointed and subjective. This judgment is ill founded, however, since the writings of many modern novelists typically are disjointed and subjective, and yet these novelists are widely held to be good writers.

Which one of the following most accurately expresses the conclusion drawn in the critic's argument?

(A) Linsey is a good songwriter.
(B) The view that Linsey is a bad songwriter is poorly supported.
(C) The writings of many modern novelists are disjointed and subjective.
(D) Many modern novelists are widely held to be good writers.
(E) Linsey's talent as a writer is no less than that of many modern novelists.

7. Computer security experts correctly maintain that computer passwords are a less secure means of protecting one's information than are alternative security options like fingerprint scanners. But computer passwords are not going to be replaced by these other options anytime soon. The alternative security options remain significantly more expensive to employ, and they can replace passwords only if they become standard on most of the world's computers.

The conclusion drawn above follows logically if which one of the following is assumed?

(A) There are ways to make computer passwords a more secure means of protecting one's information.
(B) Any security option that is no more expensive to employ than computer passwords provides less security than computer passwords.
(C) Most computer security experts do not believe that computer passwords will be replaced by an alternative security option anytime soon.
(D) Security options that are significantly more expensive to employ than computer passwords will not become standard on most of the world's computers anytime soon.
(E) As soon as a security option is developed that is not significantly more expensive to employ than computer passwords, computer passwords will be replaced as a security measure.

GO ON TO THE NEXT PAGE.

8. Statistics show clearly that in those countries with the most severe penalties for driving while intoxicated, a smaller percentage of drivers have traffic accidents involving alcohol use than in other countries. This refutes those who claim that would-be drunk drivers will not be deterred by the prospect of severe penalties.

Which one of the following would, if true, most undermine the argument?

(A) The countries with the largest populations do not have severe penalties for driving while intoxicated.
(B) Very severe penalties against driving while intoxicated are in effect only in countries in which alcohol use is rare.
(C) The higher a country's speed limits, the more frequent traffic accidents tend to be in that country.
(D) Only a relatively small minority of those who drive while intoxicated are actually apprehended while doing so.
(E) All countries impose severer penalties on those who cause accidents while driving intoxicated than on those who are merely apprehended while driving intoxicated.

9. Many airlines offer, for a fee, to "offset" the carbon emissions produced when you fly, but such schemes are almost entirely ineffective. Although the fees are usually invested in projects that directly reduce carbon emissions, in most cases these projects would have proceeded even without that investment, so no carbon emissions are prevented.

Which one of the following principles, if valid, most helps to justify the reasoning in the argument?

(A) Steps that are taken in order to mitigate the harmful effects of one's freely chosen, harmful actions do not absolve one from the original harm.
(B) If an outcome would have occurred in the absence of a certain action, then the outcome was not a consequence of that action.
(C) If a company or individual gains financially from a particular action, they should not be considered morally praiseworthy for any positive consequences of that action.
(D) Measures aimed at achieving a certain outcome should only be taken when they are of demonstrable effectiveness at achieving that outcome.
(E) If a project for reducing carbon emissions does not tackle the largest source of carbon emissions, then it is of limited value in reducing such emissions.

10. Many species of plants produce nectars known as extrafloral nectories (EFNs), which are known to attract certain ants that defend the plants against leaf-eating insects. Recently, greenhouse experiments have found that jumping spiders jump onto plants with active EFNs six times more often than they jump onto plants without EFNs, and regularly eat the nectar. So, like the ants, jumping spiders apparently defend EFN-producing plants against leaf-eating insects.

Which one of the following, if true, would most strengthen the argument above?

(A) For many species of nectar-producing plants, productivity is increased when a plant is protected from leaf-eating insects.
(B) In field experiments, the introduction of jumping spiders into an environment was followed by a significant increase in the population of EFN-producing plants.
(C) Some species of EFN-producing plants cannot survive without some outside agent protecting them from leaf-eating insects.
(D) Experiments with types of spiders other than jumping spiders suggest that these other types of spiders do not defend EFN-producing plants.
(E) Regions with large populations of ants also tend to have large populations of EFN-producing plants.

11. When using a manufactured pattern to make clothing, a tailor alters the pattern to accommodate any future distortion of the fabric. Also, unless the clothing is to be worn by a person whose measurements precisely match the pattern size, the tailor alters the pattern to fit the wearer exactly. Thus, a professional tailor never blindly follows a pattern, but always adjusts the pattern to fit the wearer exactly.

The conclusion follows logically if which one of the following is assumed?

(A) Most manufactured patterns do not already accommodate the future distortion of fabrics that shrink or stretch.
(B) At least some tailors who adjust patterns to the wearer and to the fabrics used are professional tailors.
(C) The best tailors are those most able to alter patterns to fit the wearer exactly.
(D) All professional tailors sew only for people whose measurements do not exactly match their chosen patterns.
(E) A professional tailor can always estimate exactly how much a fabric will shrink or stretch.

GO ON TO THE NEXT PAGE.

12. Typically, a design that turns out well has gone through many drafts, each an improvement over the previous one. What usually allows a designer to see an idea's advantages and flaws is a sketch of the idea. The ways in which the sketch appears muddled or confused tend to reveal to the designer ways in which the design has been inadequately conceptualized.

    The statements above, if true, most strongly support which one of the following?

    (A) The designs that turn out best go through the most drafts.
    (B) Many good designs have emerged from design ideas that were flawed.
    (C) Designs that do not turn out well have not gone through many drafts.
    (D) Designs whose initial conceptualization was inadequate rarely turn out well.
    (E) A designer will never see advantages and flaws in a design idea without the aid of a sketch.

13. Mayor: Some residents complain that the city has no right to require homeowners to connect to city water services, even though we are doing so in order to ensure public health and safety. But they are wrong. We will charge the homeowners a fair market price for the service, and our plan will benefit all of the city's residents by increasing city revenue and by making the city a healthier and safer place in which to live.

    Which one of the following principles, if valid, would most help to justify the reasoning in the mayor's argument?

    (A) A city has the right to require homeowners to connect to city water services if it charges a fair price for the service and if the requirement will benefit all the city's residents.
    (B) A city should require homeowners to connect to city water services only if it will increase revenue and make the city a healthier and safer place in which to live.
    (C) A city has no right to require homeowners to connect to city water services if it does not charge the homeowners a fair market price for the service.
    (D) Residents of a city have no right to complain about the requirement that homeowners connect to city water services if the requirement will benefit all of the city's residents.
    (E) A city can successfully increase revenue and make itself a healthier and safer place to live only if the city is able to require homeowners to connect to city water services.

14. Deborra: The art of still photography cannot enable us to understand the world. After all, understanding starts from refusing to accept the world as it looks and inquiring into the world's reality, and the reality of the world is not in its images but in its functions. Functioning takes place in time and must be explained in time; only that which narrates can enable us to understand.

    Which one of the following is an assumption on which Deborra's argument depends?

    (A) Artists who take still photographs do not attempt to understand the world.
    (B) The functioning of the world cannot be captured on film.
    (C) The art of still photography is not narrative.
    (D) A complete understanding of the world is not attainable through art.
    (E) Images cannot be properly explained.

15. Candidate: In each election in the last ten years, the candidate who supported property tax reform received a significant majority of the votes in the northeastern part of my district. In no other part of my district has there been any discernible pattern of voting for or against property tax reform. Therefore, in order to attract additional voters in the northeastern part of my district without alienating voters elsewhere, all I need to do is to go on record as favoring property tax reform.

    The reasoning in the candidate's argument is most vulnerable to criticism on the grounds that the candidate

    (A) would not attempt to enact property tax reform if elected
    (B) draws opposite conclusions about voting patterns in different parts of the district
    (C) draws a general conclusion about patterns of voting based on a small sample
    (D) surmises from the fact that two phenomena are correlated that one causes the other
    (E) draws a conclusion based solely on data that are ten years old

GO ON TO THE NEXT PAGE.

16. In an effort to boost milk production, some dairy farmers are treating cows with a genetically engineered hormone called BST. Consumer groups have opposed the use of BST even though the milk of BST-treated cows is identical in nutritional value to that of untreated cows; the treated cows run a greater risk of infection and hence are more likely to be given antibiotics, which may show up in their milk. In high levels, these antibiotics may be harmful to humans. Yet the milk of treated and untreated cows alike is regularly screened for antibiotics.

Which one of the following is most strongly supported by the information above?

(A) Consumer groups have no legitimate reasons for opposing the use of BST.
(B) Milk from BST-treated cows is as safe for human consumption as that from untreated cows.
(C) There is no advantage to the use of BST on dairy cows.
(D) Milk from BST-treated cows can be presumed safe for humans only if it is successfully screened for high levels of antibiotics.
(E) The only threat posed by drinking milk from cows treated with BST is high levels of antibiotics.

17. Legislator: University humanities departments bring in less tuition and grant money than science departments. But because teaching and research cost significantly less in the humanities than in the sciences, humanities departments bring in more money than they spend while the reverse is true of science departments. As a result, contrary to the typical characterization that humanities departments freeload on science departments, humanities departments actually subsidize science departments. Thus, it is a mistake for universities to cut humanities departments when facing budget shortfalls.

Which one of the following most accurately describes the role played in the legislator's argument by the claim that teaching and research cost significantly less in the humanities than in the sciences?

(A) It is offered as support for the accuracy of an alleged stereotype.
(B) It is an alleged stereotype rejected in the argument's overall conclusion.
(C) It is put forward as a component of an explanation for a premise of the argument.
(D) It is an intermediate conclusion from which the argument's overall conclusion is inferred.
(E) It is one of many claims each presented as independent support for the argument's overall conclusion.

18. Certain changes in North American residential architecture after World War II are attributable mainly to the increased availability and affordability of air-conditioning. Soon after World War II, many builders found that air-conditioned houses lacking the high ceilings and thick walls that traditionally kept residents cool during extreme heat generally sold well.

Which one of the following, if true, most seriously weakens the argument?

(A) High ceilings and thick walls enable houses to withstand many types of severe weather that are common in North America.
(B) Thin-walled, low-ceilinged houses are more costly to heat in winter than thick-walled, high-ceilinged houses.
(C) Houses with low ceilings and thin walls were prevalent in North America even where there was no demand for residential air-conditioning.
(D) Thin walls allow cool, air-conditioned air to escape more readily from houses than do thick walls.
(E) Soon after World War II, new thermal-insulating technology was widely applied in house building.

19. McKee: Heckling the performer is a long-standing tradition of stand-up comedy. The performers know this and learn to respond entertainingly. That's why it's unwise for comedy venues to prevent audience members from heckling.

Chapman: Heckling is only a long-standing tradition of comedy because it's tolerated. And it's usually only fun for the heckler. In most cases, heckling is just a distraction from the performance.

McKee's and Chapman's statements indicate that they disagree about each of the following EXCEPT:

(A) Comedy venues should tolerate audience members' heckling the performers.
(B) Stand-up comedians' responses to heckling should be considered part of their stand-up comedy performance.
(C) The best stand-up comedians are able to respond entertainingly when they are heckled by audience members.
(D) Many audience members at comedy venues enjoy watching stand-up comedians respond to heckling.
(E) It is unwise for comedy venues to disregard long-standing traditions of stand-up comedy.

GO ON TO THE NEXT PAGE.

20. Political scientist: Democracy depends on free choices, and choices cannot be free unless they are made on the basis of well-reasoned opinions. In the Information Age, reading skills have become essential to forming well-reasoned opinions. Thus, in the Information Age, a highly literate society will be a democratic one.

The political scientist's reasoning is flawed in that it

(A) mistakes necessary conditions for sufficient conditions
(B) fails to take into account that there are many means of forming well-reasoned opinions
(C) confuses the means of doing something with the reasons for doing it
(D) generalizes too hastily from one type of case to another
(E) takes for granted that a condition under which something occurs is a condition under which all its prerequisites occur

21. All of the students at Harrison University live in one of two residence complexes, either Pulham or Westerville. Although just a small fraction of the classes at Harrison are night classes, 38 percent of Harrison students take at least one night class. That figure is lower for Harrison students living in Westerville: Only 29 percent of those students take at least one night class.

If the statements above are true, which one of the following must also be true?

(A) More than 38 percent of the students at Harrison who live in Pulham take a night class.
(B) More than 50 percent of the students who take night classes at Harrison are from Pulham.
(C) More students at Harrison live in Westerville than live in Pulham.
(D) Harrison students living in Pulham are less likely than those living in Westerville to take more than one night class.
(E) Night classes at Harrison have larger enrollments, on average, than day classes do.

GO ON TO THE NEXT PAGE.

22. The universe as a whole necessarily tends toward greater disorder, or entropy. From this alone, it follows that the earth's biosphere has always been moving toward increased disorder as well, in spite of appearances to the contrary.

Which one of the following is most similar in its flawed reasoning to the argument above?

(A) Wooded Lake is one of the most beautiful lakes in the world. This follows from the fact that the extensive system of interconnected lakes of which Wooded Lake is a part is one of the most beautiful systems of its type worldwide.

(B) This has been the coldest April in this region in the last half-century. So, on any given day this April, it is likely that the weather was unseasonably cold.

(C) The manifest indicates that every deck on that cruise ship houses some commercial cargo, even though on some decks the cargo storage areas are difficult to find. Hence every deck on the ship is devoted to commercial cargo storage, even though this is not immediately obvious.

(D) Although Hopper claims to have been working in another part of the plant when the accident occurred, company records show that every person on the cleanup crew of which Hopper is a member was in the grain area at the time. Hence Hopper either has misremembered events, or is not telling the truth.

(E) Two of the seven critical parts in that gear assembly are unsafe to use, even though this is not obvious upon a casual inspection. The assembly therefore is unsafe to rely on and ought to be repaired.

23. Researcher: Consumption of turmeric, a basic ingredient in curry dishes, probably slows cognitive decline. Our research team analyzed a database of information about the cognitive function, ethnicity, and diet of elderly residents of Singapore. Those who eat curries regularly had higher scores on cognitive-function tests than those who rarely or never eat curries; this relationship was strongest for the elderly Singapore residents of Indian ethnicity.

Which one of the following, if true, most strengthens the researcher's explanation of the research team's findings?

(A) Even before analyzing the database, the researchers had hypothesized that turmeric consumption slows cognitive decline.

(B) Highly educated residents of Singapore are more likely than other residents to eat curries regularly.

(C) Most Singapore residents who are of Indian ethnicity eat curries regularly.

(D) Singapore residents, on a per capita basis, eat curries more often than do residents of most other countries.

(E) Indian curries generally contain much more turmeric than other curries contain.

GO ON TO THE NEXT PAGE.

24. A theory cannot properly be regarded as empirical unless there is some conceivable observation that, if the theory were false, would refute it.

The principle above most helps to justify which one of the following?

(A) Since no one was present at the origin of the universe, the Big Bang theory of the universe's origin is not an empirical theory.
(B) Since set theory is not an empirical theory, there is no conceivable observation that would refute it.
(C) Psychoanalysis is such a flexible theory that no conceivable observation could show it to be false, so it is not an empirical theory.
(D) There are conceivable observations that would refute quantum theory, so quantum theory is an empirical theory.
(E) The theory of relativity must be true since, although scientists have conceived of observations that would refute it, it has not yet been refuted.

25. Shopkeeper: Our city will soon approve the construction of a new shopping center, but I won't be relocating my store there. My store needs to be in a high-visibility site with good growth potential, but the new shopping center will be at either Maple Street or West Avenue. The Maple Street site lacks visibility, and the West Avenue site has poor growth potential.

The pattern of reasoning in which one of the following arguments is most similar to the shopkeeper's pattern of reasoning?

(A) Appiah will not renew the lease on her apartment unless her rent does not increase and she is permitted to get a pet. But Appiah's landlord prohibits pets and plans to raise the rent on every apartment in the building. So Appiah will not renew her lease.
(B) Professor Myers is unable to teach any class next semester unless it meets in Diaz Hall in the afternoon. Myers can teach either ethics or political theory. Ethics classes cannot meet in the afternoon, but political theory classes can. Political theory classes can also meet in Diaz Hall. So Myers will teach political theory next semester.
(C) Finch will not travel this month unless he can get inexpensive plane tickets or stay with a friend. But Finch only wants to travel to Bridgeport or Hazleton. Plane tickets to Bridgeport are expensive. Finch cannot stay with a friend in Hazleton. So Finch will not travel this month.
(D) The concert will not sell out of tickets unless it is held at a small venue in the downtown area. But the concert will either be held at Jensen Arena, which is a large venue, or at Pembroke Hall, which is located outside the downtown area. So the concert will not sell out.
(E) The new park near the river will not be popular unless it is well lit and its natural scenery remains undisturbed. The park will be well lit if lamps are installed near the riverbank. But installing lamps there would disturb the park's natural scenery. So the new park will not be popular.

STOP

IF YOU FINISH BEFORE TIME IS CALLED, YOU MAY CHECK YOUR WORK ON THIS SECTION ONLY.
DO NOT WORK ON ANY OTHER SECTION IN THE TEST.

Acknowledgment is made to the following sources from which material has been adapted for use in this test:

Stephen Bottomore, "Rediscovering Early Non-Fiction Film" in *Film History*. ©2001 by John Libbey.

Guy Deutscher, "Does Your Language Shape How You Think?" in *The New York Times*. ©2010 by The New York Times Company.

Rochel Gelman and C. R. Gallistel, "Language and the Origin of Numerical Concepts" in *Science*. ©2004 by American Association for the Advancement of Science.

David J. Lazerwitz, "The Flow of International Water Law: The International Law Commission's Law of the Non-Navigational Uses of International Watercourses" in *Indiana Journal of Global Legal Studies*. ©1993 by Indiana University School of Law.

Mary Mycio, "Chernobyl Paradox" in *Natural History*. ©2006 by Natural History Magazine, Inc.

Laura Sivitz, "When the Chips Are Down" in *Science News*. ©2000 by Society for Science & the Public.

COMPUTING YOUR SCORE

Directions:

1. Use the Answer Key on the next page to check your answers.
2. Use the Scoring Worksheet below to compute your raw score.
3. Use the Score Conversion Chart to convert your raw score into the 120–180 scale.

Scoring Worksheet

1. Enter the number of questions you answered correctly in each section.

	Number Correct
SECTION I	_____
SECTION II	_____
SECTION III	_____
SECTION IV	_____

2. Enter the sum here: _____
   This is your Raw Score.

Conversion Chart
For Converting Raw Score to the 120–180 LSAT Scaled Score
LSAT Form 0LSA141

Reported Score	Raw Score Lowest	Raw Score Highest
180	100	101
179	99	99
178	98	98
177	—*	—*
176	97	97
175	96	96
174	95	95
173	94	94
172	93	93
171	92	92
170	91	91
169	90	90
168	88	89
167	87	87
166	85	86
165	84	84
164	82	83
163	80	81
162	79	79
161	77	78
160	75	76
159	73	74
158	71	72
157	69	70
156	67	68
155	65	66
154	63	64
153	61	62
152	59	60
151	57	58
150	55	56
149	54	54
148	52	53
147	50	51
146	48	49
145	46	47
144	45	45
143	43	44
142	41	42
141	40	40
140	38	39
139	37	37
138	35	36
137	34	34
136	32	33
135	31	31
134	30	30
133	29	29
132	28	28
131	27	27
130	26	26
129	25	25
128	24	24
127	23	23
126	22	22
125	21	21
124	—*	—*
123	20	20
122	19	19
121	18	18
120	0	17

*There is no raw score that will produce this scaled score for this form.

ANSWER KEY

SECTION I

1. A
2. C
3. D
4. C
5. B
6. C
7. D
8. D
9. B
10. C
11. E
12. B
13. C
14. D
15. A
16. B
17. D
18. A
19. A
20. D
21. D
22. C
23. B

SECTION II

1. A
2. B
3. B
4. B
5. C
6. B
7. D
8. D
9. B
10. C
11. E
12. E
13. A
14. A
15. A
16. B
17. B
18. C
19. A
20. E
21. E
22. D
23. D
24. C
25. D
26. B

SECTION III

1. A
2. D
3. B
4. C
5. B
6. B
7. D
8. C
9. C
10. B
11. D
12. A
13. E
14. E
15. D
16. C
17. E
18. A
19. E
20. B
21. D
22. B
23. B
24. C
25. E
26. A
27. B

SECTION IV

1. E
2. D
3. D
4. E
5. D
6. B
7. D
8. B
9. B
10. B
11. D
12. B
13. A
14. C
15. D
16. D
17. C
18. C
19. C
20. A
21. A
22. A
23. E
24. C
25. D

LSAT® PREP TOOLS

The Official LSAT SuperPrep II™

SuperPrep II contains everything you need to prepare for the LSAT—a guide to all three LSAT question types, three actual LSATs, explanations for all questions in the three practice tests, answer keys, writing samples, and score-conversion tables, plus invaluable test-taking instructions to help with pacing and timing. SuperPrep has long been our most comprehensive LSAT preparation book, and SuperPrep II is even better. The practice tests in SuperPrep II are PrepTest 62 (December 2010 LSAT), PrepTest 63 (June 2011 LSAT), and one test that has never before been disclosed.

With this book you can
- Practice on genuine LSAT questions
- Review explanations for right and wrong answers
- Target specific categories for intensive review
- Simulate actual LSAT conditions

LSAC sets the standard for LSAT prep—and SuperPrep II raises the bar!

Available at your favorite bookseller.

LSAC.org